Treasures of the Taylorian:
Cultural Memory 3

'Dangerous Creations': Papers from a Roundtable Discussion

Edited by Aoife Ní Chroidheáin

Series editor: Henrike Lähnemann

Taylor Institution Library, Oxford, 2022

First published in 2022 by Taylor Institution Library

Copyright © Taylor Institution Library 2022

http://www.bodleian.ox.ac.uk/taylor

Cover image shows details from posters created during the poster workshop (see page 75)

Typesetting by Emma Huber

ISBN 978-0-9954564-8-8

Taylor Institution Library, St Giles, Oxford, OX1 3NA

Contents

Acknowledgements
Aoife Ní Chroidheáin

This publication is based on the 'Dangerous Creations' roundtable discussion, poetry reading and exhibition which took place in New College and the Taylor Institution Library on 8th April 2022.

There are several people and organisations without whom this roundtable event and book would not have been possible. I would like to thank the Oxford in Berlin Partnership, the Leverhulme Doctoral Training Centre, the Taylor Institution Library, the Bodleian Library (particularly colleagues in the Bibliographical Press), the Faculty of Medieval and Modern Languages, and New College, all of whom supported the project in various ways. I am grateful for the support of Emma Huber. Her kind encouragement and behind the scenes preparation for the exhibition was most helpful. I would also like to acknowledge and thank Alexandra Lloyd, not only for her thoughtful mentorship and support over the years, but also for helping me prepare this volume for copy-editing.

Thanks are also due to family, friends and colleagues for unfailing support and assistance, both on the day of the roundtable and behind the scenes. I would especially like to thank my conference assistants: Clíodhna Ní Chroidheáin, Ailbhe Ní Chroidheáin and Maximilian Lau for all their help with logistics and organising.

I am grateful to all the contributors within and beyond Oxford. Special thanks must go to the poets and artists who have been generous with their time and so sharing of their work and expertise.

Above all I wish to thank my doctoral supervisor Karen Leeder, whose leading research in GDR literature has been an inspiration throughout this project and to whom this book is dedicated.

Aoife Ní Chroidheáin, Oxford, 16 May 2022

Foreword

Karen Leeder

In 1986, when I began my doctorate on the work of the youngest generation of poets in the GDR, that work was pretty much unknown in the West. What was later dubbed the 'Prenzlauer Berg Connection' (Adolf Endler), was an art, music and literature scene that had developed in East Germany, giving voice to a generation largely excluded from the highly regulated official public sphere of the socialist state. Although there were such movements in many of the larger cities, it was the name of a rundown quarter of Berlin that became an unofficial label for the alternative culture that had developed. In East Germany the advent of this phenomenon was viewed largely with incomprehension, though critics Ingrid and Dieter Hähnel were not far wrong when they signalled it as 'längst nicht mehr nur eine Wohngegend, sondern eine Haltung'.[1] The fact remains, however, that 'Prenzlauer Berg' was and remains a metaphor.[2] For a long time it stood for a bohemian, avant-garde existence apparently founded beyond the deadlock of state-sponsored culture and critical dissidence. It seemed for a while to offer an enclave, an enclosed and fruitful 'Biotop' (Leonard Lorek). But later, after the revelations about the activities of the Staatssicherheit, this sphere morphed in the popular imagination into a 'Dichtergarten des Grauens' (Jan Faktor) or even a 'Schrebergarten der Stasi' (Wolf Biermann).

In truth, as has become clear since, the boundaries between this underground sub-culture and the official culture were never clear-cut and some writers seemed to be able to move between the different worlds. In the last years of the GDR several writers could even be published in Gerhard Wolf's 'Außer der Reihe' series with

---

[1] Ingrid and Klaus Dieter Hähnel, 'Junge Lyrik am Ende der siebziger Jahre', *Weimarer Beiträge*, 9 (1981), 126–54 (p. 129).

[2] Compare *Prenzlauer Berg: Bohemia in East Berlin?* ed. by Philip Brady and Ian Wallace, *German Monitor*, 11 (1995).

the prestigious Aufbau Verlag. Equally, it was soon apparent that older, established writers sponsored, inspired and even protected some of those younger writers who took part. Finally, in retrospect, it is clear that, rather than a collective literary endeavour, the initiatives that took place there were individual and fragmented. What is more, they developed considerably over the decade or so that they were in existence involving several so-called generations.

But, returning to Oxford in the 1980s, I had come to know some of this poetry almost by chance; finding proper access to this world was much more difficult, not to mention getting hold of material, whether that was books by young writers who were permitted to publish, or indeed the magazines themselves. A trip financed by the Britain–GDR Friendship Society, based down in Seven Sisters Road, allowed me to meet some of the poets in person. A later visit funded by the DAAD sent me to all the best bookshops looking for the texts. When I presented a reading list at the Brecht Buchhandlung in Chausseestraße, well known as a place to find what was not available elsewhere, the assistant looked bemused and replied along the lines of: yes, we would like to read these too. At that time, it was a case of patiently ordering books when they became available in the library of the Humboldt University, and copying out sections, or viewing the so-called 'Unikate', the original one-off graphic magazines that had been sold to West German archives and making frantic notes. The Taylor Institution Library, under German Librarian Jill Hughes, was unfailingly helpful. Through her support I managed to source much of what I needed, and the library now boasts a collection of books associated with the phenomenon, which probably cannot be bettered anywhere outside Germany. That includes some of the magazines themselves: copies of Berlin-based *Entwerter/Oder* from the mid-1980s, for example, or the more international UNI/vers(;) from the last days of the GDR and after.

Back then, I was writing as history took place, always playing catch up. When I began, the poets I was studying were the first generation 'born into' the established socialist state ('hineingeboren', to borrow the title of Uwe Kolbe's 1980 collection that first gave a name to their experience). By the time my thesis came out as a book, they were the last generation of authors to have come to adulthood in the GDR.[3] The GDR had ceased to exist and with it the parameters that governed their lives and their work. What is more, the status of several of the writers and the notion of an autonomous literature of any kind had itself had been called into question by the revelation that key figures, among them charismatic guru of the underground Sascha Anderson, had been acting as 'Inoffizielle Mitarbeiter' (IMs), in the employ of the East German Staatssicherheit. All this fed into high-level critical discussions about what literature in East Germany had been and what literature in the Berlin Republic could or should be.

When I reread by own work now, I am struck by how the study of this chapter of cultural hsitory led me to some of the most fundamental questions about the function of literature and judgment of its value. My conclusions were, and perhaps had to be, tentative: everything was so raw and recent. Certainly, several of those writers I singled out as formative have indeed gone on to become significant voices the new Germany (Durs Grünbein, Uwe Kolbe and Barbara Köhler, for example), even if some later distanced themselves from what they had written in the GDR; Durs Grünbein famously calling his work in East Germany 'poetry from the bad side'.[4] I had also imagined that the whole question of what took place in that final frenetic decade of the GDR would become a staple of future work: the questions it raised were too fundamental; the historical issues too provocative; and the literature simply too good to be ignored for long. In fact, the phenomenon of the GDR 'underground' was caught in retrospective review almost as soon as it ceased to exist. Many anthologies, often put together by those who had been involved, offered accounts almost before the GDR had disappeared in the rear-view mirror: *Abriss der Ariadnefabrik* (1990), *Die andere*

---

[3] Karen Leeder, *Breaking Boundaries: A New Generation of Poets in the GDR* (Oxford: Clarendon Press, 1993).

[4] Durs Grünbein, '"Poetry from the bad side": Gespräch mit Thomas Naumann', *Sprache im technischen Zeitalter*, 122 (1992), 442-49.

Sprache (1990), *vogel oder käfig sein* (1992), or the exhibitions of independent art like *Zellinnendruck* (1990).[5] In a sense, that process has continued, driven by the periodic stocktaking initiated by high-profile anniversaries.[6]

But the shadow of the East German secret police proved to be long and had a corrosive effect on the ways in which people approached much of this work. It took some time before accounts could appear that faced the infiltration of the Staatssicherheit head on, but also found space to offer a differentiated structural re-appraisal of the literature and art itself, as in Alison Lewis's *Die Kunst des Verrats* (2003).[7] It is impossible now for these things to be separated in any meaningful sense, as indicated further in Lewis's most recent study, *A State of Secrecy: Stasi Informers and the Culture of Surveillance* (2021).[8]

What is more, the very terms we use to approach the GDR and its literary legacy have fundamentally changed in the time since those early appraisals. We can also ask new questions of ourselves as researchers about our own investment in the dreams and nightmares of the failed socialist experiment. I was struck not so very long ago,

---

[5] *Abriss der Ariadnefabrik*, ed. by Andreas Koziol and Rainer Schedlinski (Berlin: Druckhaus Galrev, 1990); *vogel oder käfig sein: Kunst und Literatur aus unabhängigen Zeitschriften in der DDR 1979-1989*, ed. by Klaus Michael and Thomas Wohlfahrt (Berlin: Druckhaus Galrev, 1992); *Die andere Sprache: Neue DDR Literatur der 80er Jahre*, ed. by Gerhard Wolf (München: text + kritik, 1990); *Zellinnendruck*, ed. by Egmont Hesse and Christoph Tannert (Leipzig: Katalog der Galerie EIGEN + ART, 1990).

[6] *Zersammelt: Die Inoffizielle Literaturszene der DDR nach 1990; eine Bestandaufnhame*, ed. by Roland Berbig, Birgit Dahlke, Michael Kämper-van den Boogart, Uwe Schoor (Berlin: Verlag Theater der Zeit/Rescherchen 6, 2000).

[7] Alison Lewis, *Die Kunst des Verrats: Der Prenzlauer Berg und die Staatssicherheit* (Würzburg: Königshausen & Neumann, 2003).

[8] Alison Lewis, *A State of Secrecy: Stasi Informers and the Culture of Surveillance* (Lincoln, NE: Potomac Books, 2021).

in a book I edited for CUP about the legacy of the GDR, how few of my colleagues were truly ready to abandon the shapes and understandings that had governed their thinking up until then.[9] I remember wondering whether it was not time for young researchers to come to it all with new eyes, or for the culture of this time to be put into different contexts. When the possibility arose to bring a Leverhulme Doctoral Centre to Oxford examining 'Publication Beyond Print', this seemed the perfect occasion to initiate a reappraisal of the magazine culture that flourished in the 1980s East Germany in precisely that spirit. I am therefore delighted that Aoife Ní Chroidhéain has taken on that challenge. These days, of course, things are very different: the writers and artists live in a country it is possible to visit; the books and magazines are accessible and available for study; and in many cases (fortunately) the magazines themselves are digitised. Without that, COVID-19 would have pretty much blighted any attempt to review their contents over the last couple of years. But also, much more work has been done in the intervening years: on mechanisms of power, on the truths and untruths of the 'Stasi files', but also on samizdat and cultures of dissidence in other Eastern bloc countries, and there is new material to review, the practice of bootleg recording, known as 'magnitizidat', associated with the magazine *Liane*, for example.

What is more, the intervening years have allowed new generations to approach the material, and new questions to find shape more clearly.[10] It is exciting to see how, funded by the Oxford|Berlin partnership, Aoife has brought scholars and creatives together to Oxford to discuss all these questions almost forty years since I was first starting to think about these things. Her 'Dangerous Creations' roundtable and exhibition has even led to new donations of magazines to the Taylor Institution, for which we are all very

---

[9] *Rereading East Germany: The Literature and Film of the GDR*, ed. by Karen Leeder (Cambridge: CUP, 2016).

[10] For example: Lukas Regler, 'Zweifach zersammelt. Die Dichtung des Prenzlauer Bergs am Literarischen Colloquium Berlin', *Sprache im technischen Zeitalter*, 59 (2021), 499–527.

grateful and which will allow work to continue in future. This volume takes the discussion further and is a fitting testament to all her hard work on this project.

Karen Leeder, Oxford, June 2022.

(incoming Schwarz-Taylor Professor of German Language and Literature)

Foreword

Ray Ockenden

When I first began teaching in Oxford, the 18-year-old East German state was still something of a *terra incognita*, especially since it had sealed itself off with a wall. Brecht had just become an author regarded as suitable for special study, but his poetry was still relatively unknown. At seminars I held with undergraduates (one of whom established personal contact with the poet Peter Huchel) we were able to explore the remarkable richness of the poetry which flourished in the German Democratic Republic, despite the constraints on writing and publishing in that country. We also pondered the considerable influence of Georg Maurer, professor at the Institute of Literature in Leipzig and admired especially the independent voice of the then controversial poet and singer Wolf Biermann. I remember giving a paper to the Conference of University Teachers of German in the 70s on the richness of GDR poetry, (including comment on Sarah Kirsch's controversial poem 'Schwarze Bohnen') and being surprised at how little these works were known. During the later 70s and early 80s interest in the literature of the GDR increased, but it was still a bold step that Karen Leeder took when she began to examine the work of the newest GDR poets. An even bolder step was her decision not to draw a line under her doctoral research when the GDR came to an abrupt end in 1989 but to explore particularly the poets associated with the 'Prenzlauer Berg' group and the later stages of that group more thoroughly. This work, together with a continuing general interest in the work of the secret police, the Stasi, forms a background to Aoife Ní Chroidheáin's doctoral thesis, which Leeder is supervising.

Ní Chroidheáin's research project, exploring different forms of creativity in the later years of the repressive East German state, inspired her to organise a day-long conference to discuss the production of literature in a repressively controlling system. She decided to widen the scope of discussion by including art magazines as well as poetry, and by inviting Ann Komaromi, an expert on

Soviet Russian 'samizdat', to give a paper on that topic as a constructive reference point. Komaromi's paper sounded what would become a crucial theme of discussions throughout the day: artists operating in repressive regimes will explore possibilities of expression beyond simply the combating of that repression, a reminder that art is itself always seeking to burst thematic, formal and stylistic boundaries. State censorship is a political act, and combating it is thus also political; but artistic creativity is ultimately independent of such constraints.

Image: Prof. Ray Ockenden participating in the roundtable discussion

Although much of the roundtable discussions focussed on the functioning of censorship and the activity of the Stasi, broader issues were also considered, such as the balance, in any system, between individuals and society. With particular regard to the GDR situation, and those working within it, it became evident that there was a significant difference between those writers and artists who experienced the vital shift between National Socialism and Communism, the foundation of a new state which explicitly turned its back on the fascist past, and younger figures who were born into the new state, for whom the term 'hineingeboren' had been coined.

As our roundtable group moved from New College in Oxford to the Taylor Institution for the last part of the day (apart from a splendidly convivial dinner together!), we were offered an exhibition of relevant artistic materials, and a poetry reading by Uwe Kolbe which Ní Chroidheáin introduced through a short conversation with the poet. Though his work as a controversialist, notably his attack on Brecht as a lasting, significant and fateful figurehead of the repressive system, has not always found resonance, Kolbe's readings of his own poetry revealed a significant voice of the 'hineingeboren' generation. One poem he read, clearly a favourite of his (and a necessarily inadequate English version of which is appended), showed him to particular advantage: a sonnet which celebrates a rare and special moment, a meeting between art and nature from which any political dimension has been banished. It served to remind us of the richness of poetry (and perhaps also of the ultimate transitoriness of politics and politicians).

Kingfisher

But was he real? Can you trust your sight?
As though the air were squabbling with the air
At margins of the real, flashed a light:
That you *did* see him makes the moment rare.

The water lay there, totally at rest;
No movement in the grasses at its back;
The healthy tiddlers flourished unoppressed
And only you had wandered off your track –

That path you took: now blocked by what occurred;
And so, not fathoming the reason, you
Wished now to wait for him; you never stirred,

Hopeful, yet fearful, and embarrassed too,
Since he who darted past you, as he flew
Had bound you here, that fleeting, lovely bird.

(Uwe Kolbe, translated R.C.O.)

Introduction

Aoife Ní Chroidheáin

Prolonged controversy about what kinds of memorial are suitable to remember the culture of the GDR, on the one hand, and revelations about the Stasi involvement of certain East German writers with the Staatssicherheit, on the other, continue to trigger public discussions about whether the reunified Germany has truly 'come to terms with' (aufgearbeitet) the legacy of East Germany's literature. This is particulary the case with East Germany's 'unofficial' scene.

'Dangerous Creations', the title of my doctoral thesis, is evocative of the excitement and sense of literary hope of the underground scene in the GDR, but also the forces ranged against it. My D.Phil. thesis, entitled 'Dangerous Creations: Power and Autonomy in East Berlin's "samizdat"', investigates the 'subversive' literary scene of the GDR in the 1980s through in-depth case studies of three individual East Berlin magazines: *Mikado*, *Liane* and *ariadnefabrik*. As my Leverhulme Doctoral Centre scholarship is focused specifically on the theme of 'Publication beyond Print', I have been working closely not just with archive material, but also with those who once created these magazines. This study examines the magazines as examples of material culture, together with textual analysis, and interviews with the magazines' creators and artists, to delineate their unique contribution to the field of literary production in the latter years of the GDR. By researching each of the magazines' literary content, and the ways in which they were produced, my thesis contributes exciting new insights into the creative self-expression of the East Berlin literary scene.

The aim of this roundtable discussion was twofold; to bring together the artists and writers with whom I had been working in order to continue discussions about the unofficial magazines of the GDR; and secondly, to venture broader conclusions about the afterlife and cultural significance of the unofficial scene today. The day-long roundtable featured six thematic panels, each consisting of a speaker followed by an open

Q&A session. The first half of the day offered a theoretical overview of unofficial creativity in the GDR and the culture of 'samizdat', while the second half of the roundtable was dedicated to the hearing from the 'Zeitzeugen', the artists and writers from East Germany's literary bohemia.

Image: Ann Komaromi

In bringing together key international scholars of the GDR unofficial scene, along with writers and artists, and researchers of Russian samizdat, the roundtable facilitated cross-cultural and inter-disciplinary dialogue as we compared the potentially transnational forms that literary creativity and subversion took in the repressive East German state.

Image: (L–R) Prof. Sara Jones, Dr Tara Talwar Windsor, Prof. Alison Lewis

The whole event was rounded off by a view from 2022 – over thirty years after the fall of the wall – in the form of a poetry reading by Uwe Kolbe at the Taylor Institution Library. Kolbe, who was previously a co-editor of unofficial magazine *Mikado* and whose career as a writer spanned the latter years of the GDR and continues today in the Berlin Republic, was excellently placed to comment on the ways in which GDR creativity found its place in reunified Germany after the *Wende* and beyond.

Image: Uwe Kolbe speaking at his poetry reading. Reading chaired by Aoife Ní Chroidheáin (pictured also)

A further dimension to the roundtable event and poetry reading was a small exhibition of Taylorian library holdings relating to the theme of the discussions. Displayed in the Main Lecture Hall of the Taylor library where the poetry reading took place, the exhibition presented works by each of the writers, artists and academic speakers involved in the conference event. The display included issues of the original 'samizdat' magazines *Liane* and *Entwerter/Oder* which had been generously gifted to the library by their editors, Heinz Havemeister and Susanne Schleyer (*Liane*) and Uwe Warnke (*Entwerter/Oder*). It also displayed, for the first time since its acquisition, the *UNI/vers(;)* magazine collection which is also housed in the Taylor Library.

Image: (L–R) Taylor Librarian Nick Hearn receives gift copy of *Entwerter/Oder* from Editor, Uwe Warnke, at special library tour organised by Aoife Ní Chroidheáin.

Overall, the works on display showcased almost 40 years' worth of artistic practice and scholarship. Building on the dynamic history of GDR studies at the University, the exhibition offered a tangible view of the scholarship to date, while also marking the beginning of the exciting new chapter of GDR literary archive-building at Oxford.

Image: Conference attendees examine the newly gifted issue of *LIANE*.

As we have seen in recent months, most especially with the war in Ukraine, culture is often at the heart of efforts to create narratives. In this context, it feels all the more important to meet at an international level, and to hold narratives up to scrutiny. Perhaps one of the most remarkable aspects of the 'Dangerous Creation' roundtable discussion was that it produced such an internationally engaged community of practice. The roundtable's aggregate of stories, perspectives, quantitative and qualitative research became its own 'dangerous creation'; an international collaboration and an unflinching testimony to the lasting power of literary and creative self-expression.

Image: Entwerter/Oder card

Part One

The Theory of Samizdat

Creative Outlets:
Collective Creativity in the Underground Literary and Artistic Cultures in the GDR

Alison Lewis

In their book on Franz Kafka, French philosophers Gilles Deleuze and Félix Guattari offer a novel way of thinking about Kafka. They begin by asking not what his writings mean but how they function, what they do and where they 'go'. Kafka's corpus is a 'writing machine' they argue, 'a rhizome, a burrow',[1] a dynamic and meandering 'network',[2] rather like an underground rabbit warren, tunnel, or couch grass. For Deleuze and Guattari, whose philosophy places entities as disparate as grass, books and human bodies on the same ontological plane, writing is a machine. It is not just *like* a machine: it *is* a machine — made up of heterogenous parts that all interconnect with one another.[3]

The idea of GDR literature as an interconnected writing machine that feels rather like a rabbit warren, not only to the researcher, has a certain appeal. To my mind non-hierarchical and non-linear metaphors such as the burrow, rhizome or creeping grass offer particularly apt descriptors of the East German *Literaturbetrieb* during the last decade of stagnation when the official literary system started

---

[1] Gilles Deleuze and Félix Guattari, *Kafka: Toward a Minor Literature*, trans. by Dana Polan (Minneapolis and London: University of Minnesota Press, 1986), p. 3.

[2] Deleuze and Guattari, p. 29.

[3] According to Arjen Kleinherenbrink, Deleuze and Guattari consider machines (like rhizomes) to be forms of multiplicity and types of assemblages. Ships, animals, hotels, circuses, books, castles, music, orchids, wasps are all machines, assemblages or rhizomes, that is, 'everything is a machine, real, contrived or imaginary' (Kleinherenbrink, *Against Continuity*, p. 17).

to unravel. It is no coincidence that images such as the maze, labyrinth or liana were used by creative producers on the periphery of the East German official system in the 1980s. Rather than dividing the literary landscape into official and unofficial literature, it might be fruitful instead to think about all acts of writing in the GDR as part of a rhizomatic formation — that is, as a horizontal decentralized system that moves below and above ground, upwards and downwards, and sometimes even in both directions. Far more than we have acknowledged, creative writing after singer-songwriter Wolf Biermann's expulsion in November 1976 was, I believe, a desperate multi-directional search for new creative outlets as well as a new language. For most creative producers in this period of stagnation, writing became a kind of 'line of flight' — a move away from orthodoxy and hierarchical structures. Authors who were admitted into the Writers Guild questioned more openly the authority of the censorship apparatus while those writers excluded from the guilds set about creating their own 'second' unofficial or alternative literature, or German brand of samizdat. These alternative spaces of creativity often provided an opportunity for the two sides of the literary system to meet, collaborate and exchange ideas.

For both underground and aboveground writers, writing as a 'rhizomatic writing machine' was a way of forging a more congenial outlet for creative expression. This could mean embracing a particular style or poetics or adopting a mouthpiece or mask in collective defiance of official gatekeepers. Like the rhizome that can put out shoots in unpredictable places, for the last decade and more, literature in the GDR became more dispersed and hybrid, and, crucially, more elusive for the regime.

In this paper I want to talk about some of these serendipitous outlets for creative expression. What we call GDR literature has recently been called into question by Roland Berbig in his book *Auslaufmodell DDR*. Berbig calls for a shift away from a focus on the author and his or her biography and a return to the archive.[4] Returning to the archive could involve, to my mind, paying greater attention to questions of sociability and how a literary life was lived. Creativity, oddly enough, is not always factored into the story of East German literature, and if it is, it tends to be cast in terms of single-author creativity rather than the work of multiple creative actors. Of course, officially, creativity was always already a collective activity in the GDR — a land that called itself totally unironically a '*Leseland*'. We know this from official programs such as the *Bitterfelder Weg*, which tried to turn factory workers into poets and poets into farm hands. What is often not acknowledged is that creativity was frequently a social activity, for instance, it was generated by sociable occasions, by readings or gatherings, at which ideas and works were shared with like-minded others.

I wanted to think about creativity less as a production process or a factory than as a collective formation that is non-linear and that operates on multiple planes. Collaboration in the broadest sense shaped all kinds of literary creativity in the GDR. It also shaped output in a negative sense at those pesky nodes where blockages occurred such as in the ministerial offices of the *Hauptverwaltung Verlage und Buchhandel* (the Main Administration for Publishing and Book Trade). Sadly, creativity was oftentimes the outcome of illicit and destructive forms of collaboration more akin to interference and sabotage. This kind of covert collective creativity could involve invisible gatekeepers like anonymous manuscript reviewers or even disgruntled Stasi informants who doubled up as blind peer reviewers.

My main focus is on typical creative outlets that emerged in underground literary cultures in the GDR in the latter half of the 1970s. I will start with the official perception of what was wrong or

---

[4] Roland Berbig, 'DDR-Literatur archiviert: Neues zu einem alten Thema', in *Auslaufmodell ‚DDR-Literatur': Essays und Dokumente*, ed. by Roland Berbig (Berlin: Ch. Links, 2018), pp. 17–44 (p. 21).

dangerous about this illicit new literary culture and conclude with an exploration of some rhizomatic aspects of the official literary culture.

In 1983, a report, written by the *Staatssicherheit* in advance of the congress of the Writers Guild, warned of the impoverishment of the official literary system. It highlighted the dangers of the 'Austrocknung' and 'Verödung' of GDR literature through the 'Auswanderung' of writers to the West. The Stasi was alarmed at the emergence of a rival 'second' literary system — a second 'eigentliche' literature that had the potential to replace officially approved production. The department of the Stasi that authored this report — the department for analysis, the HAXX/AKG (Arbeits- und Kontrollgruppe) left no doubt that the official system was under threat from prominent West German authors and oppositional *Nachwuchsautoren* in the underground. It was also threatened by writers inside the Writers Guild itself, namely by 'bekannte Schriftsteller, die in Widerspruch zur Parteipolitik stehen.'[5]

Why did this 'second' literature pose such a threat to the regime and how did it become a major challenge in such a short space of time? Moreover, if the Stasi possessed such insights into its workings why was the secret service so powerless to curb its growth? The first overview I am aware of that the Stasi compiled of the political and artistic underground stems from the end of 1981 when the HA XX/AGK registered the rise in 'feindlich-negative Kräfte' in the capital city and the regions. The main source of concern was that these forces were developing activities, organizing 'Lesungen aber auch anderen Veranstaltungen sowie privat deklarierten Zusammenkünften unterschiedlichen Charakters und auf verscheidenen Ebenen.'[6] They were using the readings as a platform to propagate and disseminate their 'sozialismusfeindlichen oder fremden Auffassungen.'[7] There were, according to this report, sixty-five readings, thirty-four exhibitions, eight concerts, ten events based on discussions and eleven cross-over or multimedia events. The main

---

[5] BStU, MfS, HA XX/AKG, vol. 1492, folio 135.

[6] BStU, MfS, HA XX/AKG, vol. 1492, folio 20.

[7] BStU, MfS, HA XX/AKG, vol. 1492, folio 20.

cities of concern were Berlin, Dresden, Gera, Erfurt, and Karl-Marx-Stadt.[8]

The report divides the events into three categories: events in state venues, events in private spaces, and events in church facilities.[9] Of these the majority took place at the time in churches. The Stasi report distinguishes between events with and without discussion and with or without participants from the West. Some fifteen towns and cities were listed where these readings were occurring. What was especially galling for the Stasi was the fact that the reading in apartments were being organized as private initiatives and purported to have a private character. Private events were thus being used to propagate hostile-negative views.

As this report underscores, the danger stemmed from the intentional and illicit repurposing of places and spaces. Youth clubs, churches, galleries, open air settings and private dwellings were being utilized by people to disseminate potentially dangerous views and as a means of associating freely with others like themselves. Quite spontaneously, it would seem, the next generation of writers and artists had stumbled upon a sustainable answer to the intractable problem of the ever-more restrictive nature of state-controlled cultural spaces. The solution to the problem was not to be found in remodelling the public sphere, which was still in the firm grip of the party, but in repurposing the private. This was worrying for the authorities since it broke down the public-private divide and used the private sphere as a second, freer semi-public space. The master of disguises itself, the Stasi, was disturbed by the possibility that the organizers might be using deception and spoke of 'Täuschung staatlicher Organe über die Zielstellung sowie den Inhalt und Charakter.'[10] Moreover, these were spaces the state had little access to, places that the surveillance panopticon could not readily see or

---

[8] BStU, MfS, HA XX/AKG, vol. 1492, folio 22.
[9] BStU, MfS, HA XX/AKG, vol. 1492, folio 38.
[10] BStU, MfS, HA XX/AKG, vol. 1492, folio 20.

reach, despite opening surveillance checks and operations on most of the participants.

The next point of concern that the Stasi report lists in the 1982 report relates to the fact that these events were made possible by exploiting a loophole in the law. Using churches and private apartments meant that official channels for holding an event or an exhibition could be bypassed. This obviated the need to apply for a permit to hold such an event. Or as this report states, such events occurred through 'Umgehung/Unterlaufung gesetzlicher Bestimmungen',[11] although of course there was no such requirement to seek permission to invite twenty or more people to your apartment to discuss literature or art.

A further concerning aspect was that these private activities were gathering followers through largely unchecked private channels of dissemination. The organizers were deemed to be resorting to subterfuge to promote the events by labelling them 'Geburtstagsfeiern, Klassentreffen u.a.'[12] They were advertised through the use of word of mouth, or 'Flüsterpropaganda', as it is called in this Stasi report, and by 'Plakatierungen', namely posters, or 'gezielte Einladungen bzw. persönliche Einladungen', namely targeted invitations or personal invitations.[13]

By eschewing the public sphere altogether, writers were forming their own bohemian and at times, anarchic subcultures that were frustratingly out of reach for the authorities.[14] This unofficial culture was rapidly gaining momentum, morphing into a counter or competing public sphere or counter public.[15] It was in danger of

---

[11] BStU, MfS, HA XX/AKG, vol. 1492, folio 20.

[12] BStU, MfS, HA XX/AKG, vol. 1492, folio 21.

[13] BStU, MfS, HA XX/AKG, vol. 1492, folio 21.

[14] See Birgit Dahlke, 'Underground Literature?: The Unofficial Culture of the GDR and its Development after the Wende', in *Rereading East Germany: The Literature and the Film of the GDR*, ed. by Karen Leeder (Cambridge: Cambridge University Press, 2015), pp. 160–179 (pp. 161–162).

[15] See Robert Asen and Daniel C. Brouwer, 'Introduction: Reconfigurations of the Public Sphere,' in *Counterpublics and the State*, ed. by Robert

becoming a second 'eigentliche' literature, not only because virtually an entire new generation of writers was propelling it, but because older generations were joining in as well. Prominent writers such as Heiner Müller were regulars at readings as well as loyal writers such as Christa Wolf who occasionally attended the salon of Ekkehard and Wilfriede Maaß. Both Maaß' archive (now online) as well as the Stasi's document the comings and goings of well-known figures from the guilds as well as international writers from the SU and the USA. The 1982 report includes names such as Franz Fühmann, Stefan Heym, Christa Wolf, Elke Erb and Volker Braun, who are alleged to be among the participants of the happenings. While some like Heiner Müller or Stefan Heym had long since fallen foul of the regime, others such as Christa Wolf still had their roots firmly planted in the official literary system. Nonetheless, her occasional presence in these settings lent the scene cultural capital and gravitas. Others such as Gerhard Wolf and Fühmann performed important functions as 'go-betweens' between the Writers Guild, the Ministry for Culture and the 'underground'.

Another concern was that the readings were accompanied by an illegal publication culture. Poets, writers, photographers, and graphic artists were taking matters into their own hands and devising self-publishing and self-exhibition methods that since the late 1970s were successfully bypassing the censors.[16] Above all, they took advantage of loopholes in art printing regulations which stipulated that only print-runs over one hundred copies needed approval. This meant that not only did the art and the photographs need no permit if reproduced in small numbers, neither did the texts that were included among the woodcuts or screen prints. Poets joined forces with graphic artists producing limited edition, hand-bound art books that soon became collectors' items. Self-publishing of various kinds took off around the country. Some initiatives consisted of unique typescripts that were handed around and added to, while others were

---

Asen and Daniel C. Brouwer (Albany, NY: State University of New York Press, 2001), p. 7.

[16] Dahlke, p. 162.

reproduced in small print runs of between twenty and fifty copies. All consisted of combinations of media and involved creative collaborations, like the early examples *Entwerter/Oder* (1982) and *Mikado oder Der Kaiser ist nackt*. Self-publishing ventures like these evolved over the next decade as the print-runs grew and newer printing technology became available.

The salons and the samizdat publications formed part of a rapidly expanding rhizomatic creative culture that the state anxiously watched expand. Moreover, soon Lutheran churches joined in, using their internal information news channels to publish cultural artefacts, which sometimes had print-runs of between 200 and 1000 copies.

Although the Stasi was quick to collect intelligence on the happenings, it found itself largely powerless to stop them. The Stasi's main means of control was to try and infiltrate the networks and prevent them in advance or neutralize them from within. However, the report in 1982 offers a sober assessment of the Stasi's successes in this regard. It highlights the lack of regional informants to keep the subcultures under surveillance. We now know that the Stasi was only successful in recruiting two long-standing IMs who infiltrated the milieu — namely Sascha Anderson and Rainer Schedlinski. Despite their attempts to meddle in everything, they had only a small part of the underground covered. Anderson in particular had little interest in having his own initiatives wound back and pressed on regardless. To be sure, the Stasi could arrest or intimidate the organizers, as it did occasionally. Arrests however harboured the risk of *Dekonspiration*, namely that the Stasi moles would be exposed, which was to be avoided at all costs.

In a centrally planned socialist state, culture was structured hierarchically by a strict system of streamlined gatekeeping, starting with the guilds involving the publishers right through to the ministries for culture and state security, all of whom acted as filters and brakes to the free flow of creativity. By the mid to late 1970s blockages in this creative process no longer meant literary production or undesirable manuscripts merely disappeared. Instead, writers invented alternatives outlets and creative offshoots for them, often at great cost. These creative lines of flight moved mainly underground sweeping up writers, artists, and intellectuals in a host of semi-legal activities that bypassed the gatekeepers altogether, forming a kind of rhizomatic writing machine that was constantly in flux. This machine connected not only younger writers with established ones, but it also reached out to diplomats, western journalists, and academics as well as to West German publishers such as Rotbuch Verlag. The spread was multidirectional, vertical, and horizontal, East to West and West to East, and it occurred in multiple cities at the same time. As the 1982 Stasi report I quoted at the start makes clear, the surveillance of informants was insufficient to keep the broad range of activities in check. And where the Stasi's moles managed to have an impact — say, in preventing an alternative writers' guild and depoliticizing the artistic and literary underground — the literary rhizome simply regenerated itself elsewhere. Thus, the expansion of subcultural activities continued throughout the 80s, with the underground gaining more momentum, and as it swept up more creatives in its flow while gradually becoming more openly political. The final irony is that in 1988, just as the regime was about to implode, the official system opened its gates tentatively to underground poets when Gerhard Wolf was permitted to publish some of them in a new series '*Außer der Reihe*' with Aufbau. But this went unnoticed because a year later there were far bigger gates soon about to be opened.

Select Bibliography

Bundesbeauftragter für die Unterlagen der Staatssicherheit der ehemaligen DDR (BStU), MfS, HA XX/AKG, vol. 1492.

Dahlke, Birgit. (2015). 'Underground Literature?: The Unofficial Culture of the GDR and its Development after the *Wende*', in *Rereading East Germany: The Literature and the Film of the GDR*, ed. by Karen Leeder (Cambridge: Cambridge University Press), pp. 160-179.

Deleuze, Gilles and Félix Guattari. *Kafka: Toward a Minor Literature,* trans. by Dana Polan (Minneapolis and London: University of Minnesota Press, 1986).

Kleinherenbrink, Arjen. *Against Continuity: Gilles Deleuze's Speculative Realism* (Edinburgh: Edinburgh University Press, 2019).

Soviet Samizdat: Creating Alternative Social Spaces

Ann Komaromi

Soviet samizdat — when it is known to readers today — is likely to evoke thoughts of celebrated works by Alexander Solzhenitsyn such as *The Gulag Archipelago* and *First Circle*. Such works have much literary interest, but they also possess clear political significance arising from Solzhenitsyn's portrayal of the Stalinist prison camp system. Taken together with the highly publicized struggle to defend human and civil rights by Andrei Sakharov and other Soviet dissidents in the 1970s, such works suggest that samizdat is primarily a political phenomenon, comprised of heroic individuals challenging the Soviet regime.

This is a reductive view, but it has been surprisingly persistent. Of course, the understanding of samizdat as a political phenomenon owes much to Cold War policies and practices: the U.S.-government sponsored organization Radio Liberty began to assemble the first and largest collection of Soviet samizdat in 1968. By 1971, the Radio had created a Samizdat Section to research, classify and publish samizdat texts, making them available for western scholars and policy analysts.[1] Radio staff also broadcast items by shortwave radio for listeners in the Soviet Union. Their samizdat collection subsequently dominated the research landscape for many years. Radio Liberty collected items with strategic relevance and political interest: belletristic and other artistic or cultural texts were not included in the published series. Many years after the end of the Soviet Union, many studies still took the published collection to be comprehensive.[2] Scholars, including those contesting the character and significance of samizdat and

---

[1] The published series from Radio Liberty were Sobranie dokumentov samizdata (Collection of Samizdat Documents), 1972-1978; and Materialy samizdata (Materials of Samizdat), 1975-1991.

[2] Gordon Johnston, 'What Is the History of Samizdat?' *Social History*, 24. 2 (1999), 115-33.

dissidence, continued to take the political reading as the basis for discussion. Two landmark studies, Serguei Oushakine's analysis of samizdat and Alexei Yurchak's description of the last Soviet generation, usefully challenged binary oppositions associated with the Cold War; however, as they did so, they downplayed the significance of phenomena they saw primarily in political terms.[3]

In fact, the much fuller range of sources on samizdat and independent activity available today resists the idea that samizdat and unofficial activity was primarily a political phenomenon for most of those involved. We now have plenty of studies on the cultural underground, which draw attention to the special social dynamics of unofficial behavior and socializing.[4] To put it simply, we have shifted our attention from a focus on the vertical axis between citizens and the regime and learned to take seriously the meaning of the horizontal axis among citizens engaged in independent activity.

Samizdat studies today may take a new sort of literary starting point, asking what the samizdat status of works meant for the author and the reader as they met at the site of the unauthorized text. Relatedly, we can inquire what it meant for a work to be produced and to circulate as samizdat — this includes asking what kind of relationship it had to the official Soviet context, knowing that this was not fixed and that it changed over time. We may also interrogate samizdat objects from an artistically informed sociological perspective: to wit, how does the text signify via its materiality? In sum, we may ask about the function of samizdat in creating new alternative social spaces.

---

[3] Serguei A. Oushakine, 'The Terrifying Mimicry of Samizdat', *Public Culture*, 13.2 (2001), pp. 191-214; Alexei Yurchak, *Everything Was Forever, until It Was No More: The Last Soviet Generation* (Princeton: Princeton University Press, 2006).

[4] See, for example, Steiner; Bolton; *Dropping Out*; Smola; *The Oxford Handbook of Soviet Underground Culture*; Komaromi.

Samizdat – New Relations Between Authors and Audiences

Our knowledge of samizdat now exceeds any one archive and takes into account the array of collections, published sources, press reports along with participant testimony in memoirs and interviews about the existence and function of samizdat. Samizdat journals have provided one way to turn the focus to groups and publics. The Project for the Study of Dissidence and Samizdat at the University of Toronto Libraries features a comprehensive database of Soviet Samizdat Periodicals from the years 1956–1986, as well as a set of fully digitized issues of a couple of dozen literary and art journals not published during the Cold War.[5]

Samizdat is a poetic and parodic neologism that entered dictionaries in many languages as a term referring to a system of informal textual production and circulation operating outside of the tightly controlled network of official institutions in the Eastern bloc in the late twentieth century. The term 'samsebiaizdat' was coined by poet Nikolai Glazkov, who self-published (*sam sebia izdal*) his poetry at home in typescript copies, taking other jobs for income and work status. The term gained currency in slightly different form, as 'samizdat', among young creative intelligentsia in Moscow around the end of the 1950s – beginning of the 1960s. Historian Aleksandr Daniel' conceptualized samizdat as a 'mode of existence of the text'.[6] This meant that samizdat did not refer to a certain type of (oppositional) content. Instead, it was any text produced and shared outside institutional control. This was typically done in the USSR by handwriting or (more often) typing copies. Works published in pre-revolutionary times or works published abroad could be reproduced

---

[5] The Project for the Study of Dissidence and Samizdat, hereafter PSDS, includes digital copies of originals held at the Research Centre for East European Studies at Bremen University.

[6] Daniel', 'Istoki i smysl sovetskogo Samizdata', in *Antologiia samizdata*, vol. 1, pp. 17–33, p. 17.

(often by using a photographic camera) and shared hand to hand –
this was samizdat, too. People remember copying and sharing poems
that were hard to get – by poets Anna Akhmatova, Osip
Mandel'shtam, Boris Pasternak, Marina Tsvetaeva and others –
already in the 1940s in what became a relatively widespread practice
in the 1950s and 1960s.

Later people shared new uncensored poetry by Joseph Brodsky,
Natalia Gorbanevskaia, and others. The poetry collection series
Syntax (*Sintaksis*, 1-3, 1959–60) was one early landmark.[7] In
addition, samizdat journals, texts and hand-bound collections were
important for the people who gathered at the Maiakovskii
monument in Moscow, which opened on July 28, 1958. The site
became known as the Maiakovka, and the people who gathered there
between 1958 and 1961 for informal poetry readings and socializing,
were called the Maiakovtsy. People made acquaintances and formed
networks relevant for further independent activity: future rights
activists mixed with future advocates of a Russian national revival.
Many had a strong interest in art and poetry. One of the most famous
of the Maiakovtsy was Iurii Galanskov, who edited the samizdat
collections called *Phoenix* (Feniks, 1961), and *Phoenix-66* (1966).
Other poetic collections, such as "Chu!", *Bumerang*, and others, were
not published.[8]

Rights activism – the main activity to which the term 'dissidence'
pointed – became important in the late 1960s. In September of 1966,
the Presidium of the Supreme Soviet of the RSFSR passed article 190-
1 on the dissemination and preparation of false statements slandering
Soviet society (*Biographical Dictionary*, p. 653). This new article

---

[7] Daniel', 'Istoki i smysl sovetskogo Samizdata', in *Antologiia samizdata*,
vol. 1, pp. 17-33, p. 17.

[8] Polikovskaia, Liudmila, *My predchuvstvie … predtecha … Ploshchad'
Maiakovskogo.1958–1965* (Moscow: Zven'ia, 1997); *Antologiia samizdata:
Nepodtsenzurnaia literatura v SSSR. 1950-e–1980-e*, 3 vols., ed. by V.V.
Igrunov and M.Sh. Barbakadze (Moscow: Mezhdunarodnyi institute
gumanitarno- politicheskikh issledovanii, 2005), p. 35.

(passed along with Article 190-3, concerning unauthorized assembly that disturbed the peace), aimed to deal with the spontaneous demonstration, open letters and other uncensored texts produced in response to the arrest and trial of Siniavskii and Daniel'. At the same time, the Siniavskii-Daniel' affair set off a new phase of unofficial communication by Soviet citizens with foreign correspondents and diplomats who were interested in uncensored reporting and writing and who helped send it abroad.

Literary samizdat did not recede with the rise of rights activism; in fact, it became more prominent in the 1970s as part of an autonomous cultural sphere. Other types of independent activity thrived, as well. The encyclopedic reference work *Samizdat of Leningrad* provides a broad and detailed look at the unofficial cultural movement in Leningrad.[9]

The year 1976 saw the emergence of two important literary journals: *Thirty-Seven* (Tridtsat' sem' 1–21, 1976–81) was one of them.[10] It featured a religious-philosophical orientation along with outstanding poetry. The journal *The Clock* (*Chasy*, 1976–90; no. 1–80) was more capacious and eclectic.[11] Large issues running to hundreds of pages appeared regularly every two months featuring a wide variety of texts ranging across poetry and prose, cultural criticism, visual arts, philosophy, theatre, music and more.

The physical space of the journals corresponded to the different kind of social space they projected: *Thirty-Seven* was slimmer and less

---

[9] *Samizdat Leningrada, 1950-e–1980-e: Literaturnaia entsiklopediia*, ed. by V. E. Dolinin, B. I. Ivanov, B. V. Stanin, and D. Ia. Severiukhin (Moscow: Novoe literaturnoe obozrenie, 2003).

[10] *PSDS*, https://samizdatcollections.library.utoronto.ca/islandora/object/samizdat%3A37. See Von Zitzewitz, *Poetry and the Leningrad Religious-Philosophical Seminar*; and Von Zitzewitz, *The Culture of Samizdat*, particularly pp. 125-148.

[11] *PSDS*, https://samizdatcollections.library.utoronto.ca/islandora/object/samizdat%3Achasy.

regular. It was associated with small seminars, primarily Tat'iana Goricheva's Religious-Philosophical Seminar. The editors described the journal in the foreword to the first issue as 'a necessary continuation of our friendly socializing'. The editors of *Thirty-Seven* also proclaimed, the "flat spirit of opposition is not capable of inspiring any one of us'. They insisted, 'Render unto God the things that are God's (*Bogu dolzhno otdat' Bozh'e)'.*[12] The journal provided a slim and fragile platform for connecting the small fellowship with an ideal world culture in Osip Mandel'shtam's sense.

The Clock offered a wider space, accommodating as much variety within unofficial culture as possible — provided the texts were not anti-Soviet. Boris Ivanov and his fellow editors solicited contributions from first-time as well as experienced authors. As a result, the large and regular issues of *The Clock* helped demonstrate to Soviet officials that such activity was too widespread to be easily controlled. A better solution — advocated by editors of *The Clock* — would be a physical space for independent culture established with the knowledge and acquiescence of the authorities. The first meeting of an officially allowed independent literary and cultural organization called Club-81 took place in the Dostoevsky Museum in November 1981.[13] Subsequent Club events and samizdat publications facilitated the development of independent — but carefully legal — culture.

Interesting independent culture was not confined to Leningrad. The samizdat folio series *Moscow Archive of New Art* (*MANI*, 1-4, 1981-1982) provided a space for gathering and discussing works by conceptualist artists, the majority of whom were in Moscow.[14] Andrei Monastyrskii edited the first folio. Envelope seven in that first

---

[12] 'The Leningrad Underground Continues to Operate', *Tridtsat' sem'* 5 (1976) images 158-59 in *PSDS*.

[13] 'Klub-81', *Samizdat Leningrada*, pp. 410-413.

[14] Alexandra Danilova and Elena Kuprina-Lyakhovich, 'MANI: An Experiment in Modelling Cultural Space', ed. by Margarita Tupitsyn, Victor Tupitsyn, and David Morris, trans. Mikhail Grachev, in *Anti-Shows: APTART 1982-84* (London: Afterall Books, 2017), p. 241.

issue contained documentation of an art action called 'White Cube' (*Belyi kub*, 1980) created by Natal'ia Abalakova and her husband Anatolii Zhigalov, who together formed the collective 'TOTART'.[15] The action consisted of constructing an 'Ideal Space' (a white cube) within the artists' apartment out of thin wooden beams, white bandages, chalk, coal and paper clips. Spectators became participants helping to wrap the large frame (530 x 300 x 250 cm), which, when completed, filled the room from side to side and top to bottom, dividing the group into two. Participants cut through the Cube to come together again, the used bandages were rolled into a ball and placed in the centre of a mandala drawn by Zhigalov on the floor where the Cube had been.[16]

The whole action required a few hours. The use of an ideal geometric shape (the cube) and pure color (white) to construct an environment in real space recalls both Suprematism and Constructivism from the avant-garde heritage. The playful character of the action and the eclecticism of the traditions invoked (with the addition of the Mandala), helps locate this in the neo-avant-garde of the late twentieth century. The apartment environment and collective of participants is distinctive for the Soviet underground: Ekaterina Bobrinskaia observed, "The avant-garde strategy is unexpectedly found in an everyday situation'.[17]

Considered in terms of alternative social space, the construction of the cube suggests the possibility for making – and destroying and re-making – the group's context. The ideal space blocking passage through the apartment invites reflection on the construction and

---

[15] Natalia Abalakova and Anatoly Zhigalov, *TOTART* (Moscow: Maier, 2012).

[16] Description and images of the performance can be found in Abalakova and Zhigalov, p. 16; and at 'White Cube', https://conceptualism.letov.ru/TOTART/WHITE-CUBE.htm.

[17] Ekaterina Bobrinskaia, 'TOTART Natal'i Abalakovoi i Anatoliia Zhigalova: Performansy', in: N. Abalakova, A. Zhigalov, *TOTART: Russkaia Ruletka* (Moscow: Ad Marginem, 1998), p. 47.

transgression of boundaries mentioned in essays by the couple: this includes the division between the artist and the viewer, the boundary between art and everyday life, as well as the difference between utopian vision and real social and practical needs. Nonconformist art, like the samizdat publications in which it is reflected, provokes critical reflection on the space for creative, critical and contemplative activity in Soviet society. By this time, in the late 1970s- early 1980s, people were undertaking such activity in their own lived contexts and on their own terms.

If the phenomenon of Moscow Conceptualism was relative elite, other types of samizdat culture were not. Samizdat rock zines — which were very numerous and widespread by the early 1980s — offered event calendars, reviews of albums and shows, and essays on the development of Soviet rock music (Kushnir). Rock music occupied something like a 'gray zone' on the margins of official Soviet culture. It was partially tolerated and therefore accessible to people in smaller and provincial cities around the Soviet Union. Rock 'zines helped create a distinct social ethos, an imagined place that welcomed everyone who 'got it' (McMichael). This was an alternative social space that was accessible, a space placed at an angle to regular Soviet society.

Conclusion

The implications of samizdat texts cannot be entirely accommodated within models that put civil society in opposition to the state, nor can they be fully addressed with a focus on individuals. We also need to think through what it means for collectives of readers and writers to use informal textual production and circulation to create alternative social spaces.

It is certainly the case that samizdat in the Soviet Union was not always political or oppositional. Research since the Cold War has revealed a more highly diversified samizdat alternative public sphere than we might have realized from early efforts at documentation and diffusion of samizdat documents in the west. Alongside activism designed to document and publicize rights abuses (which drew a lot of attention abroad), people pursued the possibility of independent cultural expression and social activity. Such endeavours had their origins in the general Soviet context of questioning and relative freedom of the post-Stalin era. However, as time went on, many opted not to address the regime or official policies, or even western readers — a decision to avoid direct political engagement that was motivated by strategic but also principled reasons. In the samizdat of the cultural underground, people first of all addressed their peers Of course, there were remarkable individual authors and works that came out of the Soviet underground scene. However, the proliferation of this type of activity suggests a kind of social creativity — a *poiesis* of publics and their social space – that expands our sense of its significance.[18]

Bibliography

Abalakova, Natalia and Anatoly Zhigalov, *TOTART* (Moscow: Maier, 2012)

Antologiia samizdata: Nepodtsenzurnaia literatura v SSSR. 1950-e– 1980-e, 3 vols., ed. by V.V. Igrunov and M.Sh. Barbakadze (Moscow: Mezhdunarodnyi institute gumanitarno-politicheskikh issledovanii, 2005)

Biographical Dictionary of Dissidents in the Soviet Union, 1956-1975, Edited by S.P. de Boer, E.J. Driessen and H.L. Verhaar (The Hague: Martinus Nijhoff Publishers, 1982)

Bobrinskaia, Ekaterina, 'TOTART Natal'i Abalakovoi i Anatoliia Zhigalova: Performansy', in: N. Abalakova, A. Zhigalov, *TOTART: Russkaia Ruletka* (Moscow: Ad Marginem, 1998), pp. 47-48

---

[18] Michael Warner, *Publics and Counterpublics* (New York: Zone Books, 2002), p.114-15.

Bolton, Jonathan, *Worlds of Dissent: Charter 77, The Plastic People of the Universe, and Czech Culture under Communism* (Cambridge, MA: Harvard University Press, 2012)

Danilova, Alexandra and Elena Kuprina-Lyakhovich, 'MANI: An Experiment in Modelling Cultural Space', ed. by Margarita Tupitsyn, Victor Tupitsyn, and David Morris, trans. Mikhail Grachev, in *Anti-Shows: APTART 1982–84* (London: Afterall Books, 2017), pp. 232-244

Dropping Out of Socialism: The Creation of Alternative Spheres in the Soviet Bloc, ed. by Juliane Fürst and Josie McLellan (Lanham, MD: Lexington Books, 2017)

Johnston, Gordon, 'What Is the History of Samizdat?' *Social History*, 24. 2 (1999), 115-33

Komaromi, Ann, *Soviet Samizdat: Imagining a New Society* (DeKalb, IL: Northern Illinois University Press, 2022)

Kushnir, Aleksandr, *Zolotoe podpol'e. Polnaia illiustrirovannaia entsiklopediia roksamizdata. 1967–1994. Istoriia. Antologiia. Bibliografiia* (Nizhny Novgorod: Dekom, 1994)

McMichael, Polly, McMichael, '"After All, You're a Rock and Roll Star (At Least, That's What They Say)": *Roksi* and the Creation of the Soviet Rock Musician', *Slavonic and East European Review*, 83.4 (2005), 664-84

Oushakine, Serguei A. 'The Terrifying Mimicry of Samizdat', *Public Culture*, 13.2 (2001), 191-214

Project for the Study of Dissidence and Samizdat, ed. by Ann Komaromi (Toronto: University of Toronto Libraries, 2015). http://samizdatcollections.library.utoronto.ca

The Oxford Handbook of Soviet Underground Culture, ed. by Mark Lipovetsky, Ilja Kukuj, Tomáš Glanc, Maria Engström, and Klavdia Smola (New York: Oxford University Press, 2021)

Polikovskaia, Liudmila, *My predchuvstvie . . . predtecha . . . Ploshchad' Maiakovskogo. 1958-1965* (Moscow: Zven'ia, 1997)

Samizdat Leningrada, 1950-e–1980-e: Literaturnaia entsiklopediia, ed. by V. E. Dolinin, B. I. Ivanov, B. V. Stanin, and D. Ia. Severiukhin (Moscow: Novoe literaturnoe obozrenie, 2003)

Smola, Klavdia, 'Community as Device: Metonymic Art of the Late Soviet Underground', *Russian Literature*, 96–98 (2018), pp. 13-50

Steiner, Peter, 'On Samizdat, Tamizdat, Magnitizdat and Other Words That Are Difficult to Pronounce', *Poetics Today*, 29. 4 (2008), 613-28

'TOTART', *Moscow Conceptualism: Russian Conceptual Art*, https://conceptualism.letov.ru/TOTART/TOTART.htm

Von Zitzewitz, Josephine, *Poetry and the Leningrad Religious-Philosophical Seminar, 1974- 1980: Music for a Deaf Age* (Cambridge: Legenda, 2016)

——. *The Culture of Samizdat: Literature and Underground Networks in the Late Soviet Union* (London: Bloomsbury Academic, 2020)

Warner, *Publics and Counterpublics*, (New York: Zone Books, 2002)

Yurchak, Alexei. *Everything Was Forever, until It Was No More: The Last Soviet Generation.* (Princeton: Princeton University Press, 2006)

Literature as Knowledge: Samizdat and Underground Revelation

Sara Jones and Tara Talwar Windsor

Since the opening of the Stasi files in 1992, we have learned in detail what the Stasi wanted to know and from whom, and the mechanisms by which they collected that information. However, we know far less about what GDR citizens knew about the methods of the Stasi and what coping strategies they developed to circumvent the intrusion in their lives. What happens if, rather than asking what the Stasi knew about those living in the GDR, we ask what GDR citizens knew about the Stasi and how that knowledge was conveyed and transmitted? What role did literature play in the production and communication of knowledge about the Stasi? What was the potential of fiction to function as a form of knowledge in an authoritarian society in which the public sphere was tightly controlled?

Two key concepts frame our response to these questions: *secrecy* and *knowledge*. The existence of the Stasi, their infiltration of the private and public spheres, was known in the GDR, but not in full and not openly: the activities of the Stasi might thus be designated a 'public secret', something that is both known and unknown.[1] The tactics of the Stasi in the literary sphere — for example, the recruitment of IMs and open observation — meant that in their efforts to find out the secrets of their subjects, the Stasi were required to reveal some of their own. On the other hand, GDR writers were the supposed purveyors of *Ersatzöffentlichkeit*; and yet, literature by its nature works with metaphor, allusion, allegory and poetic language which both reveals 'truths' and conceals them.

---

[1] Michael Taussig, *Defacement: Public Secrecy and the Labor of the Negative* (Stanford: Stanford University Press, 1999).

But what does 'knowledge' mean in relation to literary fiction? Literature might function as a 'medium of knowledge':[2] a process through which knowledge is shared and constructed. Indeed, many literary scholars work with what John Gibson describes as a 'humanist intuition'; that is the 'thought – or hope – that literature presents the reader with an intimate and intellectually significant engagement with social and cultural reality', but that it does so through a vision of '*other* worlds'.[3] And yet with this 'humanist intuition' we put faith in the idea that fiction – which makes no claim to extra-textual referentiality – might in fact be referential to something extra-textual. Gibson's book is an effort to resolve this impasse by conceptualising literature as playing 'a crucial role in the construction of those narratives in virtue of which we give sense to our characteristically human practices and experiences'.[4] Gibson conceives of literature as an archive of 'standards of representation' of cultural forms by virtue of which we can say '*this* is jealousy, *this* is anger, *this* is suffering' and have a shared understanding of what is meant[5] – or in our context, 'this is life in a state dominated by secrecy', 'this is paranoia', 'this is suspicion', 'this is trust'.

If we combine Gibson's insights with the position that knowledge is also situated – 'indissolubly social'[6] – then we need to add that the 'shared understanding' of those 'standards of representation' is only created in context and through communication. Literature can only function as knowledge in any sense if it is read and the form that readership takes determines the nature of the knowledge produced. To function as knowledge in the way intended by the author, the

---

[2] Fredrik Barth, 'An Anthropology of Knowledge', *Current Anthropology*, 43.1 (2002), 1–18 (p. 3).

[3] John Gibson, *Fiction and the Weave of Life* (Oxford: Oxford University Press, 2007), p. 2.

[4] Gibson, p. 50.

[5] Gibson, pp. 70-73. Emphasis in original.

[6] Andreas Glaeser, *Political Epistemics: The Secret Police, the Opposition, and the End of East German Socialism* (Chicago: University of Chicago Press, 2011), p. 163.

literary text must meet with an 'adequate reader' who is able to understand the particular use of language deployed to convey that knowledge.

Literary production in the GDR provides the ideal site to explore this proposition, as its readership was structured not only by the vagaries of the literary market, but also by censorship, state control and the availability of a second audience in a radically opposed political and social system. An interesting case study here is that of Uwe Kolbe's poem 'Kern meines Romans', which contained within it, as an acrostich, a 'hidden' poem that was highly critical of the state and party. The first letter of each capitalised word spells out the following:

Eure Maße sind Elend

Euren Forderungen genügen Schleimer

Eure ehemals blutige Fahne bläht sich träge zum Bauch

Eurem Heldentum den Opfern widme ich einen Orgasmus

Euch mächtige Greise zerfetze die tägliche Revolution[7]

However, cracking the code required an 'adequate reader'; the publication history of this text shows that it did not always meet with one. A Stasi report dated 4 May 1982 states that on submission to the anthology *Bestandaufnahme 2,* Kolbe's work was read by different informants, as well as lectors in the publishing house. None recognised the 'feindlich-negative Aussagen in Kolbes Machwerk'.[8] In a file note dated 11 May 1982, we are told that the publisher had

---

[7] Uwe Kolbe, 'Kern meines Romans', in *Bestandsaufnahme 2: Debütanten 1976-1980*, ed. by Brigitte Böttcher (Halle/Leipzig: Mitteldeutscher Verlag, 1981), pp. 82–83.

[8] Bundesarchiv (BArch), MfS AOP 1082/91 Bd.10, p. 28.

learned about the hidden poem from 'Leserkreisen an den Buchhandel'; another file note dated 18 May 1982 points directly to a reader who returned the book to their local library, demanding to know why such a work was allowed to circulate The Stasi files contain records of meetings with leading functionaries such as Klaus Höpcke, who quite clearly understood who were the targets of Kolbe's poetological attack.[9] With his poem, Kolbe revealed knowledge, in Gibson's sense, about the repressive atmosphere in the GDR – a 'standard of representation' about what it was like to exist as a young writer in an authoritarian state. At the same time, he conceals that knowledge in a way that requires an adequate reader to uncover it.

How does this work in the case of samizdat literature? The editors and authors of samizdat texts worked on the assumption that – despite concealing their activities from a broader public – they would find adequate readers who would understand and appreciate their works, not least on the basis of shared experiences and points of reference.[10] These forms of unofficial literary production offered considerable scope for openness, or for bolder experimentation with revelation and concealment. At the same time, those underground, counter-publics were also subject to (more or less) intense surveillance by the Stasi and its informants, so that the Stasi also became part of the audience for these works.

One good example is Bernd Wagner's satirical short story 'Wie Tute bis zum HSV durchkam', written in 1983 and published in the underground journal *Mikado* in 1985, before appearing in two West

---

[9] BArch, MfS AP 10820/92, pp. 57-83.

[10] Uwe Kolbe, Lothar Trolle and Bernd Wagner, 'Mikado 1-12. Ein Vorwort', in *Mikado oder Der Kaiser ist nackt: Selbstverlegte Literatur in der DDR*, ed. by Uwe Kolbe, Lothar Trolle and Bernd Wagner (Darmstadt: Luchterhand, 1988), pp. 9-10.

German anthologies in 1986 and 1987.[11] The text is prefaced with a motto quote from the 25th canto of Dante's inferno — 'Es reckte, als er schwieg, der Dieb die Hände mit durchgesteckten Daumen beid empor' (p. 100) — and a note, capitalised and enclosed in parentheses, that the ensuing story had been overheard in the 'Grosse Concordia' pub in Weissensee. The main tale is then told by a first-person narrator, Tute, in strong Berlin dialect, about the time he penetrated the Stasi's security barrier and managed to meet the players from the Hamburger Sportverein football club after they had played a match against BFC Dynamo, the East Berlin team sponsored by the Stasi (and other state institutions).

Tute concocts a plan to force his way past the uniformed 'Schutzengel' wearing 'Anzüge grüne Schlipse gelbe Hemden und Parteiabzeichen' (p. 101) and into the hotel lift. Delighted to find the Hamburg players in the bar, Tute proposes a toast to the West German team: '"Na dann erst ma Prost auf euren Sieg über die Stasis. Ich kann euch garnich sagen wat mir das für eine Genugtuung is"' (p. 102). Having secured a signed shirt to prove to his friends that the story wasn't invented, Tute recounts how he left the hotel triumphantly with a conspicuous parting shot at the guards in the foyer; the obscene hand gesture directed to God in Dante's original, now directed at the supposedly omnipotent 'yellow shirts' in Tute's story.

The Stasi files suggest that, before this story was published in *Mikado*, Wagner had read a story entitled 'Wie ich zum HSV kam' at a youth club in Leipzig in September 1984 to an audience of 30 people.[12] Despite the misunderstanding of the title here, this is clearly the same Tute story and was deemed to contain 'negative und

---

[11] Bernd Wagner, 'Wie Tute bis zum HSV durchkam', in *Geh doch rüber: Begegnungen von Menschen aus Ost und West*, ed. by Per Ketman (Darmstadt: Luchterhand, 1986), pp. 100–104, and in Wagner, *Ich will nicht nach Österreich* (Darmstadt: Luchterhand, 1987), pp. 131–136. In-text references to 1986 version.

[12] BArch, MfS AP Nr. 36564/92, p. 139.

verunglimpfende Äußerungen über das MfS'.[13] A second report recognises the distance between the author and narrator-protagonist but nevertheless offers a simplistic interpretation of the text and the knowledge it conveys from the informant's point of view, namely, that the author intended to show that the Stasi officers had not only failed to stop the man reaching the HSV players, but that they were also easily recognised by their uniform clothing.[14]

Written at a time when Wagner had detached himself from the official literary scene, Tute's story reflects his own disdain for and defiance of state power. Through its publication in *Mikado*, with its circulation of 100 copies that were passed around amongst acquaintances, the text would have found a limited but not insignificant audience familiar with the images and 'standards of representation' it contains and (re-)produces: this is the omnipresence — not to mention perceived absurdity and fallibility — of a state security apparatus purporting to protect GDR citizens from the capitalist West; this is everyday resistance and individual agency.

Our second example takes us away from the realm of samizdat in the strictest sense, because the texts in question were not even published underground before their author was arrested and his writings seized by the Stasi. The author in question is Ralf-Günter Krolkiewicz, who wrote short stories and poems alongside his career as an actor and director. Krolkiewicz' readings from his literary works at unauthorised events and to students in Potsdam and Dresden had already attracted the Stasi's attention, before his last public appearance on 21 June 1984 at the youth club Spartacus in Potsdam, where he had read 21 poems and four short stories to an audience of about 90.[15] A week after this reading, the *Operativer Vorgang* 'Bühne'

---

[13] Ibid.

[14] BArch, MfS AP Nr. 36564/92, pp. 144-145.

[15] Joachim Walter, 'Ralf-Günter Krolkiewicz – Von der Einsamkeit der Welt, oder: Der fatale Wunsch dazuzugehören' afterword in *Ralf-Günter Krolkiewicz, Nirgends ein Feuer mehr* (Frankfurt a.M.: Edition Büchergilde, 2006), pp. 147–157 (p. 150).

was initiated against Krolkiewicz who was accused of 'staatsfeindliche Hetze'. After searching his apartment on 6 July 1984, the Stasi arrested him three days later. He was subsequently sentenced to 18 months in prison but was expatriated to the West after a year.[16]

Krolkiewicz' texts therefore only reached limited public audiences including the IMs who reported on him, after which they were only read by the hostile Stasi reader (until publication in 2006). According to the Stasi, Krolkiewicz' satirical short story 'Der Dissident' was a cornerstone of that last reading in Potsdam.[17] The story is a parody of the oppositional literary scene itself, as well as the aging GDR regime, its cultural functionaries and the Stasi.[18] The main protagonist, Edmund L. — a 50-year-old critical writer, still considered to be 'literarischer Nachwuchs' —, writes a hidden poem with a coded message calling for the assassination of 'unser Erster Vorsitzender' (p. 17). The secret text is decoded by a 'pfiffige Bibliothekarin' (p. 17), an adequate reader of sorts, who then tries to blackmail Edmund L. However, because he dreams of making his name as a dissident, Edmund is eager for his subversive act to be made public. Indeed, he decides to announce it himself in a café, 'in dessen unmittelbarer Nähe die Genossen der *Inneren Hygiene* leben und arbeiten und hier ihren Dienstkaffee schlürfen: Wessen Nähe übrigens ist bei uns vom Kaffeetrinken dieser Genossen verschont...': a clearly recognisable representation of the omnipresent Stasi (p. 18). Much to Edmund's dismay, though, the news breaks the following morning that the 'Erster Vorsitzender' has been exposed and executed as an agent of US imperialism, meaning Edmund's calculated attempt to get arrested as a dissident has spectacularly failed

---

[16] Ibid., p. 151.

[17] 'Eröffnungsbericht zum Operativer Vorgang "Bühne"', 28 June 1984, pp. 1–6 (p. 2), copy in Bundesstiftung zur Aufarbeitung der SED-Diktatur (StAufarb), Archiv unterdrückter Literatur in der DDR (AuL), Ralf-Günter Krolkiewicz, 43-II.

[18] 'Der Dissident' reproduced in *Krolkiewicz, Nirgends ein Feuer mehr*, pp. 17–21. Page references in main text.

and he now risks being suspected of being a '*Hygiene-Spitzel*' himself (p. 19).

Here, Krolkiewicz' satirising and fictionalising techniques function in both revelatory and concealing ways. For example, his thin veiling of the MfS as the 'Ministerium für die innere Hygiene' — sinisterly recast as a ministry responsible for internal cleanliness rather than security — is very recognisable to the reader (or listener). Moreover, it is materially visible through the handwritten edits in his typescript, which was seized by the Stasi, where we see the words 'Ministerium für Staatssicherheit' crossed through and replaced with 'Ministerium für die innere Hygiene'.[19]

The Stasi's reading of 'Der Dissident' forms a key part of the opening report of the OV 'Bühne', in which they recognise, for example, Krolkiewicz' fictionalisation of what they term 'wahre Begebenheiten', including Uwe Kolbe's hidden poem.[20] Like Wagner's Tute story, there is much in Krolkiewicz' bitingly satirical writing that draws on and generates shared knowledge about life — particularly as an artist — in an authoritarian state, the decrepit and opportunistic nature of the state leadership and its apparatus, and a lack of honesty and open discussion in the tightly controlled public sphere. Rather than finding an audience with whom he could openly discuss his critique, however, the knowledge conveyed by Krolkiewicz' texts was only that which could be gleaned by the hostile Stasi readership, who deemed them to be evidence of the writer's own dissident stance.

Kolbe's poem and the stories by Wagner and Krolkiewicz sit at different points along a spectrum of revelation and concealment that structured literary production in the GDR and authors' choices within the authoritarian system. Some works were written 'for the drawer' and read — if at all — by a limited group of friends and family.

---

[19] Original typescript in StAufarb, AuL, Ralf-Günter Krolkiewicz, 43-I.

[20] 'Eröffnungsbericht zum Operativer Vorgang "Bühne"', p. 5, StAufarb, AuL, Krolkiewicz, 43-II.

Some writers used history and myth to both conceal and reveal knowledge about the GDR and Stasi, thereby anticipating an adequate reader who could read 'between the lines'. Others opted for total revelation in their texts, which could however only be published in the West, restricting readership to an audience in a quite different social and political context. Samizdat texts could be just as revelatory as those written 'for the drawer' or those destined for publication in the West, with the difference that they were intended and did indeed find an immediate East German audience, however limited, which comprised both sympathetic readers and the potential hostile audience of the Stasi.

Bibliography

Barth, Fredrik, 'An Anthropology of Knowledge', *Current Anthropology*, 43.1 (2002), 1–18

Gibson, John, *Fiction and the Weave of Life* (Oxford: Oxford University Press, 2007).

Glaeser, Andreas, *Political Epistemics: The Secret Police, the Opposition, and the End of East German Socialism* (Chicago: University of Chicago Press, 2011).

Kolbe, Uwe, 'Kern meines Romans', in *Bestandsaufnahme 2: Debütanten 1976-1980*, ed. by Brigitte Böttcher (Halle/Leipzig: Mitteldeutscher Verlag, 1981), pp. 82-83.

Kolbe, Uwe, Lothar Trolle and Bernd Wagner, 'Mikado 1-12. Ein Vorwort', in *Mikado oder Der Kaiser ist nackt: Selbstverlegte Literatur in der DDR*, ed. by Uwe Kolbe, Lothar Trolle and Bernd Wagner (Darmstadt: Luchterhand, 1988), pp. 9-10.

Krolkiewicz, Ralf-Günter, *Nirgends ein Feuer mehr* (Frankfurt a.M.: Edition Büchergilde, 2006)

Taussig, Michael, *Defacement: Public Secrecy and the Labor of the Negative* (Stanford: Stanford University Press, 1999).

Wagner, Bernd, 'Wie Tute bis zum HSV durchkam', in *Geh doch rüber: Begegnungen von Menschen aus Ost und West*, ed. by Per Ketman (Darmstadt: Luchterhand, 1986), pp. 100-104.

——, 'Wie Tute bis zum HSV durchkam', in *Ich will nicht nach Österreich* (Darmstadt: Luchterhand, 1987), pp. 131-136.

Walter, Joachim, 'Ralf-Günter Krolkiewicz – Von der Einsamkeit der Welt, oder: Der fatale Wunsch dazuzugehören', in *Ralf-Günter Krolkiewicz, Nirgends ein Feuer mehr* (Frankfurt a.M.: Edition Büchergilde, 2006), pp. 147-157.

Archive Sources

Bundesarchiv, MfS AOP 1082/91.

Bundesarchiv, MfS AP 10820/92.

Bundesarchiv, MfS AP Nr. 36564/92.

Bundesarchiv, MfS AP Nr. 36564/92.

Bundesstiftung zur Aufarbeitung der SED-Diktatur (StAufarb), Archiv unterdrückter Literatur in der DDR (AuL), Ralf-Günter Krolkiewicz, 43-I.

Bundesstiftung zur Aufarbeitung der SED-Diktatur (StAufarb), Archiv unterdrückter Literatur in der DDR (AuL), Ralf-Günter Krolkiewicz, 43-II.

Bild 1: *LIANE* 1, Ostberlin März 1988.

Part Two:

Samizdat in Practice

Edition *LIANE*:
Eine Perspektive der Macher und Künstler. Kurze Erinnerungen und Reflexionen 2022 – der Blick zurück

Susanne Schleyer & Heinz Havemeister

Im Februar 1988 gehörten wir als Spätgründung in Berlin zur dritten Generation von selbstverlegten, inoffiziellen Zeitschriften. Wir, Susanne Schleyer und Heinz Havemeister, hatten die Idee einer Zeitschrift, nannten sie *LIANE*, und über Verwandte in West-Berlin besorgten wir uns einen gebrauchten C64 (Commodore-Heimcomputer, für uns State of the Art) samt Drucker, denn zuerst mussten die technischen Voraussetzungen geschaffen werden. Die Vervielfältigungsmöglichkeiten waren wegen des staatlichen Informationsmonopols der DDR und der Zensur bei Druckerzeugnissen selbst gegen Ende der 1980er Jahre noch sehr eingeschränkt.

Image: Schleyer & Havemeister speaking at the roundtable discussion

Wir holten uns Unterstützung und brachten als lose Gruppe von Mitherausgebern im Frühjahr 1988 die erste *LIANE*-Nummer als Versuchsballon heraus. Wir, das waren: Volker Handloik, Heinz Havemeister, Susanne Schleyer und Michael Thulin [1]

Naiv waren wir nicht, kannten etliche inoffizielle Zeitschriften und wussten, was wir nicht wollten. *LIANE* sollte ein neuer ‚unverbrauchter' Kreis von Beteiligten sein, der programmatische Ansatz nicht einfach ein Aufguss derselben Künstler und Autoren schon vorhandener Zeitschriften. Laut unseres Kalendereintrag vom 20. April 1988 war die *LIANE*-Auslieferung vom Buchbinder sogar eine Art Geburtsakt: „Liane geboren", stand da geschrieben. Zu Besuch kamen die Autoren S(c.)happy (Peter Wawerzinek), BAADER ("Matthias" BAADER Holst) und Volker (Handloik) als 'Geburtsbeschauer'. Warum *LIANE*? Der Name bezeichnet eine Kletterpflanze und gefiel uns wegen seiner Mehrdeutigkeit. Einen gedanklichen Hintergrund bildete die Schrift *Rhizom* von Gilles Deleuze und Félix Guattari.[2] Das vernetzende Sinnbild der Lianen unterscheidet sich von der hierarchischen Struktur des Baumes, mit der wir schon als Kinder beim Malen oder Zeichnen in der Schule konfrontiert worden sind und die uns womöglich geprägt hat.

Die holzige Kletterpflanze als andere Strukturschablone ist ein Kompass, mit dem man die starre Bezogenheit von oben und unten verlassen kann — heute würden wir es 'Netzwerk und Vernetzung' nennen. Und dazu mit einem Frauennamen zu kokettieren, war gerade im Umkreis der männerbündlerischen Autoren- und Kunstszene im Prenzlauer Berg sehr amüsant. Sicher war der Name auch ein wenig von Susanne Schleyers damals meterlangen Haaren inspiriert.

---

[1] Volker Handloik (Journalist, 1961–2001), Heinz Havemeister (Musiker/Künstler und Kunstwissenschaftler, geb.1958), Susanne Schleyer (Künstlerin/Fotografin und Germanistin, geb. 1963) und Michael Thulin (Pseudonym für Klaus Michael, Germanist, geb.1959).
[2] Gilles Deleuze und Félix Guattari, *Rhizom* (Berlin: Merve Verlag, 1977).

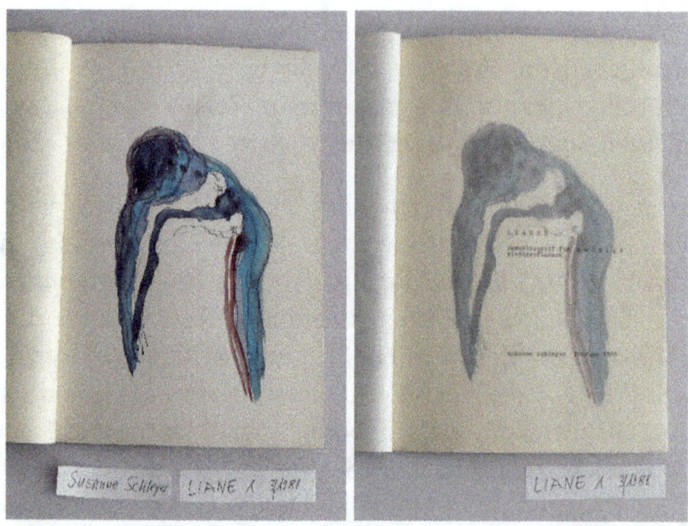

Bild 2/3: 'Lianen' von Susanne Schleyer, *LIANE* 1, Ostberlin März 1988.

Die inoffizielle *LIANE*-Produktion jenseits des staatlichen Einflussbereichs lief in der öffentlichen Wahrnehmung unter dem Radar — schon wegen der kleinen Auflage, anfänglich 20, dann 25, später 50 Exemplare und mehr. Die Umschläge waren handgefertigte Originale, sollten haptisch sinnlich wirken und riechen heute, im Jahr 2022, noch nach der verwendeten Farbe. Uns war der Originalcharakter wichtig, da man bis zu einer Auflage von 99 Exemplaren künstlerische Werke ohne staatliche Druckgenehmigung herstellen konnte bzw. es dann kein ausdrückliches Verbot gab. Wenn die Abbildungsqualität besonders gut sein sollte, gaben wir die Originale zum Kopieren über Umwege Freunden in West-Berlin. Anderes ließen wir in einem der ganz wenigen privaten Foto(kopie)-Läden anfertigen, wenn noch etwas fototechnisch montiert werden musste. So geschehen bei dem Cover unserer Kassettenproduktion 'zwischen bunt und bestialisch: all die toten albanier meines surfbretts'[3] mit Musik und Texten von "Matthias" BAADER Holst.

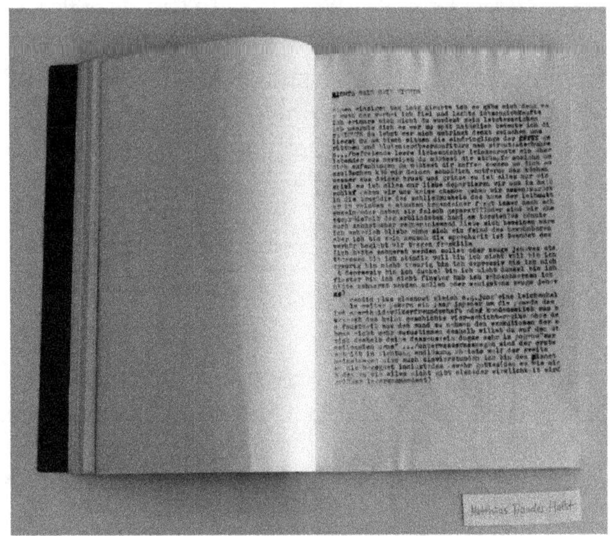

Bild 4: 'Nichts sein sein nichts' von 'Matthias' BAADER Holst, *LIANE* 2, Ostberlin Juli 1988.

Bei der Auswahl der Arbeiten favorisierten wir keinen sehr strengen Qualitätskanon, auch wenn wir einige ablehnten, was nicht immer konfliktfrei war. Das Unfertige, Prozesshafte sollte ebenso seinen Platz bekommen. Ja, es musste einen 'undefinierbaren Rest' geben. Am besten fanden wir Beiträge, bei denen der oft staatlicherseits vorgeschobene Begriff 'Qualität' von zeitgeisttreibender Originalität untergraben und von einem erfrischenden Dilettantismus überlagert wurde. Das Figurale stand neben abstrakten Motiven im Vordergrund, persönliche Befindlichkeiten wurden hier und da mittels serieller Bildstruktur gesteigert.

---

[3] 'Matthias' BAADER Holst, *zwischen bunt und bestialisch: all die toten albanier meines surfbretts*, MC (Musikkassette), Edition *Liane* 01, 1988.

Mit *LIANE* 2 (Juli 1988) hatten wir unseren ausgesuchten Hauptkreis von Autoren mit Annett Gröschner, "Matthias" BAADER Holst, Peter Wawerzinek, Mario Persch, Cornelia Klauß u. a. gefunden. Neu im Heft war die Einführung des Beilagenteils 'DDR Samplings'; 'Die Beilage DDR-Samplings verpflichtet sich einer kulturellen Spurensicherung. Es geht um die Vorstellung von verstreuten Texten, die sich mit alternativen Kunst- und Lebensformen beschäftigen.'[4] Die unmittelbare Anregung für die Wortfindung 'DDR Samplings' kam aus dem Bereich der Musik, von Heinz Havemeisters Verwendung eines Sampling Keyboards beim Musikprojekt *Heinz & Franz*.[5]

Bild 5 (links): Umschlag. *LIANE* 2, Juli 1988, Ostberlin.
Bild 6 (rechts): Umschlag. *LIANE* 3, Dezember 1988, Ostberlin.

Als dritte Zeitschriftengeneration spürten wir seismografisch vermehrt die Brüche und Phasen, die bewirkten, dass Wissen um die

---

[4] *LIANE*, Heft 2, Juli 1988.
[5] Vgl. Heinz & Franz/A.F., *Moebius: Alle Aufnahmen/Eine Auswahl*, Musikkassette (DDR: klangFarBe 007, 1988).

eigene Subgeschichte verloren ging.[6] Viele Leute gingen in 'den Westen'. Ein. Durch Beschlagnahmungen staatlicher Behörden der DDR verschwand 'Subkulturgut'. Ein Grund, warum wir im Laufe der Zeit verstärkt thematische Hefte herausgaben.[7] Letztendlich ging es um die Vermittlung und Vernetzung verschiedener Kreise, um subkulturelle Landgewinnung. Gerade die Themen alternative Galerien,[8] DDR-Comic,[9] Musik und Tapes im Independent-Bereich waren unbestellte Felder. Neben Autorentexten konnten Bildende Künstler/Fotografen in der *LIANE* ihre Arbeiten zeigen.

Im Sinne der Spurensicherung war uns klar, dass wir in den thematischen Heften die Alternativkultur verbreiten, manifestieren und samplen mussten. Wir nahmen zu diesem Zeitpunkt die DDR schon nicht mehr ernst. Rückblickend auch eine Form von Distanzierung und (Selbst-)Archivierung. Vielleicht schon ein Abschied, von dem wir nicht wussten, dass es einer ist, dass wir die DDR, unsere eigene Subgeschichte, paradoxerweise nur noch als geschichtliches Material ansahen.

---

[6] Begriffsbeschreibung von Peter Weibel in seinem Vorwort 'Was ist und was soll eine Subgeschichte des Films?', in: Scheugl, Hans u. Schmidt, Ernst, *Eine Subgeschichte des Films. Lexikon des Avantgarde-, Experimental- und Undergroundfilms* (Frankfurt a.M.: Suhrkamp, 1974), S. 12–27.

[7] *LIANE*, Heft 5, Juli 1989 (Poetik-Materialheft), enthält unter anderem die Reproduktion der verschollenen Heft-Edition *POE SIE ALL BUM zur 'Zersammlung'*. Die 'Zersammlung' fand vom 5.3.–11.3.1984 in Berlin statt und gilt als gescheiterter Versuch, einen unabhängigen Schriftsteller-verband zu gründen.

[8] Vgl. *LIANE*, Heft 6, November 1989 ('Alternative Galerien, Wohngalerien und anderes'). Bei den selbstorganisierten Ausstellungen in alternativen (Privat-)Galerien in Wohnungen/Ateliers oder auf Dachböden ging es nicht vordergründig um den kommerziellen Verkauf von Kunst, sondern um die Herstellung von Öffentlichkeit, um ein freies Podium für Experimente zu offerieren, auf dem es keine ästhetischen und ideologischen Einschränkungen gab.

[9] Handloik, Volker, *Leichtmetall. Comics in der DDR.* (Berlin: *LIANE* 11, 1990).

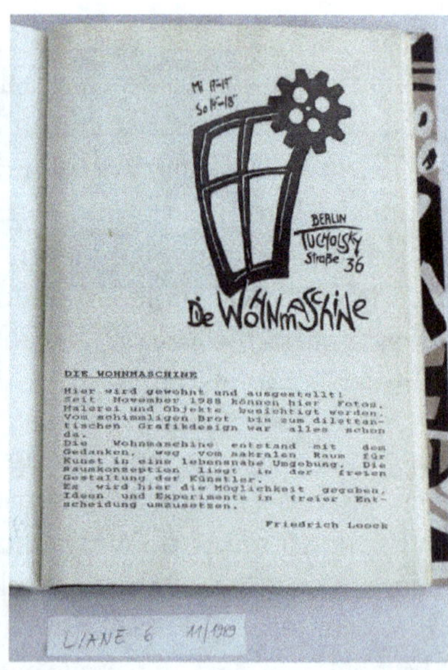

DIE WOHNMASCHINE

Hier wird gewohnt und ausgestellt! Seit November 1988 können hier Fotos, Malerei und Objekte besichtigt werden. Vom schimmligen Brot bis zum dilettantischen Grafikdesign war alles schon da.
Die Wohnmaschine entstand mit dem Gedanken, weg vom sakralen Raum für Kunst in eine lebensnahe Umgebung. Die Raumkonzeption liegt in der freien Gestaltung der Künstler.
Es wird hier die Möglichkeit gegeben, Ideen und Experimente in freier Entscheidung umzusetzen.

Friedrich Loock

Bild 7 (links): Bild von Friedrich Loock von Susanne Schleyer. *LIANE 6*, November 1989, Ostberlin.
Bild 8 (rechts): Die Wohnmaschine von Friedrich Loock. *LIANE 6*, November 1989, Ostberlin.

In *LIANE* 3 (Dezember 1988) führten wir explizit die Rubrik 'Kritik' ein, angelegt auf Austausch, auf Aktion und Reaktion. Wir wollten bewusst eine Lücke füllen, denn szeneinterne Kritik war seinerzeit noch nicht ausgeprägt und eher unüblich bzw. begann sich mal verbissen, mal humorvoll und manchmal mit ironisch-zynischen Anklängen erst zu entfalten und herauszubilden.

Ende 1988 wurde die Staatssicherheit auf uns aufmerksam. Ein IM, der Stasispitzel mit dem Decknamen 'Andreas', informierte über unsere Zeitschrift am Rande seines Berichts vom 23. November 1988 über eine andere Gruppe, die ein kirchlich-angebundenes Oppositionsblatt herausgab.[10] Man solle inzwischen bei der 3. *LIANE*-Ausgabe angekommen sein und treffe sich am 'Dichter'-Stammtisch in der Berliner Kneipe Keglerheim. Das stimmte, da dort

---

[10] Archiv *LIANE*, lose Blattsammlung.

wirklich einmal die Ausgabe der *LIANE*-Belegexemplare an beteiligte Autoren erfolgte. Außerdem wurde am 23. Februar 1989 eine einseitige 'Information zur KLEINZEITSCHRIFT *'liane'*[11] von der Hauptabteilung XX/Abteilung 9 erstellt. In der Regel war diese Abteilung für die Bearbeitung alternativer Künstler zuständig. Darunter fielen auch die selbstverlegten 'Kleinzeitschriften'. Gerade mit Hilfe eines Spitzelnetzes verschaffte man sich Zugang zur Oppositions- und alternativen Kulturszene und wollte vor allem die Etablierung einer 'zweiten Kultur' (außerhalb der staatlichen Kontrolle) verhindern bzw. einschränken.

Die 1980er Jahre waren die Hochzeit der Semiotik. Die Entdeckung, nicht nur versteckt über Zeichen zu kommunizieren — es war eigentlich ein Kampf mit Zeichen. Uns gefielen Außenseiter, und wir gefielen uns selbst als alternative Außenseiter, ähnlich wie die ostdeutschen Punks, die sich international orientiert über Kleidungscodes, Frisuren usw. vom DDR-Staat nonverbal zeichensetzend abgrenzten und sich überlebensalltägliche Freiräume eroberten. Neben der redaktionellen Arbeit sind in den *LIANE*-Heften eigene künstlerische Arbeiten und Texte der vier Mitherausgeber zu sehen bzw. zu lesen. In unseren Arbeiten spiegelt sich die Auseinandersetzung mit Zeichensystemen wider, nicht nur in den *LIANE*-Blättern der Serie '*Adam + Eva*' zu sehen.[12] Mit fiktiven, hieroglyphenähnlichen Schriftzeichen und schwarz-weißen Tusche- und Kohlezeichnungen zeigen wir die eigene Syntax, suchten und erfanden eine Sprach- und Bildwelt als fluides Gegenmodell zur starren Omnipotenz der fixierenden Machtsprache, der 'Sklavensprache',[13] um freie Spiel- und Assoziationsfelder zu erzeugen. Dazu flankiert von dem Gedanken, was wir selbst — auch im Leid — schwarz auf weiß geschrieben und gezeichnet haben, muss wichtig sein, muss Sinn besitzen. Ob es hier,

---

[11] Ebenda.

[12] Beispiel: Susanne Schleyer und Heinz Havemeister, Serie '*Adam + Eva*', gemeinsame Zeichnungen (Berlin: *LIANE* 04, März 1989).

[13] Elke Erb, *Vexierbild*. (Berlin: Aufbau, 1983), S. 57.

in unser beider Arbeiten, gesteigert im Kontrast, schwarz auf Mystik, sogar auf Coolness hinweist bzw. weiß dem Weltlichen und Körperlichen entsagt oder nur einen Anflug in die eigene Welt bedeutet, bleibt selbst ein Geheimnis. Ein häufiges gestalterisches Motiv ist das griechische Mäanderband. Das Buch *Kassandra*[14] von Christa Wolf, das Leseerlebnis, die Beschäftigung mit dieser Seherin, mit der Antike, hat sich stark eingezeichnet und Spuren hinterlassen. Und immer wieder taucht das Schmetterlingsmotiv auf, dem Verspieltheit, Wandlungsfähigkeit und Leichtigkeit nachgesagt wird, das aber auch Wiedergeburt und Neubeginn versinnbildlicht.

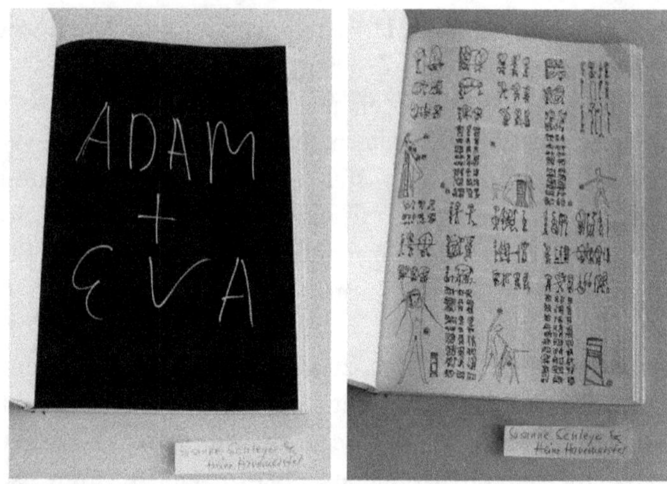

Bild 9/10: 'Adam & Eva' von Havemeister und Schleyer. *LIANE* 4, November 1989, Ostberlin.

Während der Umbruchszeit 1990 schlossen wir uns mit den Redaktionen der inoffiziellen Zeitschriften *ariadnefabrik*, *Verwendung* und *Braegen* zu einer Verlagsgemeinschaft zusammen und gründeten den Verlag Druckhaus Galrev.[15] Nach der Enttarnung zweier

---

[14] Christa Wolf, *Kassandra. Vier Vorlesungen, eine Erzählung* (Berlin, Aufbau, 1983).

[15] Der Verlagsname 'Galrev' und der Name des Verlagscafés 'Kiryl' sind Anagramme der Wörter Verlag und Lyrik und beziehen sich auf die experimentelle Literatur des Prenzlauer Bergs der 1980er Jahre.

gewichtiger Stasisspitzel im Verlag verließen wir Anfang 1993 das Druckhaus. Parallel brachten wir den schon vor dem Mauerfall geplanten Originalkatalog zur 1989er Ausstellung 'Fotografie in Aktion' heraus.[16] Wir zeigten und befragten das Medium Fotografie in verschiedenen experimentellen Zusammenhängen. Volker Handloik und Michael Thulin waren zu dieser Zeit nicht mehr dabei. Aus der 1988 schon begonnenen Musik-*LIANE* entstand 1999 das Buch 'Wir wollen immer artig sein', das die Geschichte der Punk- und Independentszene der DDR beschreibt.[17] Bis 2016 erschienen in loser Folge weitere *LIANE*-Ausgaben, darunter überwiegend originale Fotobücher und zuletzt ein Siebdruckbuch mit der Nummer 16.

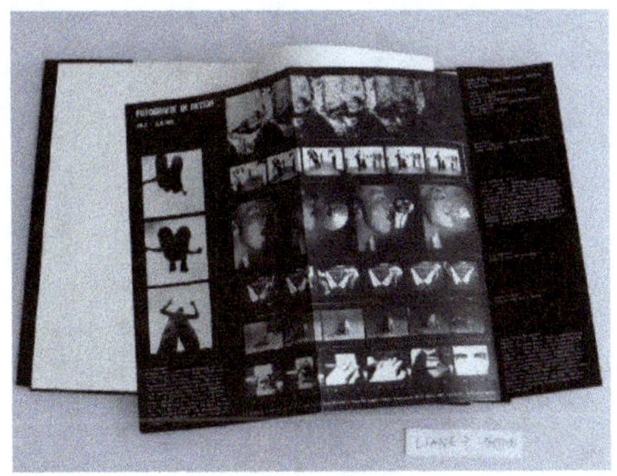

Bild 11: 'Fotografie in Aktion'. *LIANE* 7, 1989/1990.

---

[16] *Fotografie in Aktion, LIANE*, Heft 7 (1989/90). Begleitband zur Ausstellung „Fotografie in Aktion", die vom 20.7.–11.8.1989 im Haus der Jungen Talente in Berlin stattfand.

[17] Ronald Galenza und Havemeister, Heinz, *Wir wollen immer artig sein. Punk, New Wave, HipHop und Independent-Szene in der DDR 1980 bis 1990* (Berlin: Schwarzkopf & Schwarzkopf, 1999) erweitert 2005 und 2013.

Bild 1: Foto von Andreas Tesch, Berlin: 1986

ENTWERTER/ODER:
Vom Start einer 'Nicht Lizenzierten'[1] Zeitschrift zu einem Langzeitprojekt

Uwe Warnke

Als junge Studenten der Technischen Universität Dresden (DDR) wuchsen wir in der zweiten Hälfte der 1970er Jahre in eine längere Phase kultureller Stagnation hinein. Diese hatte ihren Ursprung in der Ausbürgerung Wolf Biermanns aus der DDR im November 1976.[2] Es entstand ein Protest zahlreicher Intellektueller, Schauspieler und Künstler gegen diese Entscheidung in deren Folge zahlreicher Schriftsteller, Künstler und Schauspieler die DDR gen Westen verließen. In den Verlagen herrschte daraufhin anhaltend eine Verunsicherung der jungen Generation von Autoren und allem Neuen gegenüber. Man zog sich zurück und verwaltete die Backlist. Stillstand eben.

Als Siegmar Körner und ich im März 1982 unter dem Titel ENTWERTER/ODER in Ostberlin ein Heft (15 x 21 cm) in einer Auflage von vier Exemplaren fertigstellten, ging es zunächst um etwas rein individuelles, etwas eigenes.[3] Die ersten Ideen dazu hatten wir noch in Dresden; bis zur Realisierung in Ostberlin, wo wir beide mittlerweile gelandet waren, verging noch ein Jahr. Wir wollten selbst darüber bestimmen, was mit unseren Texten geschieht. Diesen Ansatz setzten wir auf diese Weise um. Ein Wortspiel ergab den

---

[1] Diesen Begriff wählte die Staatssicherheit mit Blick auf die Zeitschrift.

[2] Politischer Liedermacher, der mit seinen kritischen Liedern die Politik und Politiker der DDR kritisierte und parodierte. Nach einem Konzert im Herbst 1976 in Köln/BRD verweigerte man ihm die Wiedereinreise in die DDR.

[3] Ab 1983 war Uwe Warnke der alleinige Herausgeber.

Titel. Ein Witz, hinter dem sich keine klare Programmatik verbarg.[4]
Die Texte wurden mit der Schreibmaschine abgeschrieben. Siegmar
Körner entwarf den Umschlag, den er als Originalzeichnung viermal
anfertigte. Buchdeckel und Inhaltsseiten wurden mit Nadel und
Faden von uns in Rückstichheftung per Hand zusammengenäht.

Bild 2: Entwerter/Oder Nr. 1, Ostberlin 1982
Gestaltung: Siegmar Körner.

Es spiegelte sich in diesem anfänglichen Tun aber auch eine gewisse
Unsicherheit; die Texte erschienen nicht unter unseren Namen,
sondern unter Pseudonymen.[5] Gleichzeitig dachte auch niemand
von uns dabei an eine Folge von weiteren Ausgaben. Von einer
'Zeitschrift' war nicht die Rede.

---

[4] In einer internen Rezension von Katrin Rohnstock im Jahr 1985 wurde
allerdings die Frage gestellt: 'Was wird entwertet und womit füllt sich das
ODER?'
[5] Details des Prozesses zu der ersten Ausgabe sind nachzulesen in: Uwe
Warnke, 'entwerter*oder / eins 1982 / 4 Exemplare / Ostberlin', in *E/O 1
Box, Faksimile der ersten Ausgabe mit weiteren Materialien* (Berlin: Uwe
Warnke Verlag, 2015).

Unsere kleine Unternehmung sprach sich schnell herum[6] und es waren die unerwartete Anerkennung, Zustimmung und die Angebote zur aktiven Mitarbeit, die ein zweites Heft sofort folgen ließen (Pseudonyme wurden hier bereits aufgegeben).[7] Und schließlich regte sich unter den jungen Künstlern der Wunsch, mit Fotografie und Grafik sich daran beteiligen zu wollen — allerdings sei das Format zu klein. So probierten wir bei der dritten Ausgabe das Format 30 x 42 cm, bis wir uns schließlich mit der vierten Ausgabe aus praktischen Gründen auf das Format DIN (Deutsche Industrie Norm (auch Deutsches Institut für Normung)) A4.[8] Ganz offensichtlich stießen wir auf ein Bedürfnis der jungen Generation ihrer Kreativität neue Wege zu eröffnen und gaben dafür den Impuls. Dabei paarte sich gesundes Selbstbewusstsein mit einer Trotzhaltung. Es darf aber auch nicht vergessen werden, dass wir durchaus viel Spaß dabei hatten. Aus einer individuellen Äußerung war innerhalb kurzer Zeit ein Periodikum geworden.[9]

Durften wir bei solch einer Publikation, die natürlich auch eine Alternative zu den ansonsten herrschenden Zensurmechanismen war, die zugesandten Texte redigieren, auswählen und eventuell ablehnen? Ist die Aussage: 'Jedes Heft ist so gut wie die zugesandten Texte und künstlerischen Arbeiten', lediglich ein Gemeinplatz, der als eine nachgereichte Erklärung für weniger gelungene Ausgaben

---

[6] Im Rückblick in den 2000er Jahren tauchte die Frage auf, wer denn den Anfang mit diesen Zeitschriften gemacht habe. ENTWERTER/ODER war die erste original-grafische Künstlerzeitschrift in der DDR! Siehe: Uwe Warnke, 'Entwerter-Material (den Umständen entsprechend)', in *Die Addition der Differenzen. Die Literaten- und Künstlerszene Ostberlins 1979 bis 1989*, herausgegeben von Uwe Warnke und Ingeborg Quaas (Berlin: Verbrecher Verlag, 2009), 94-103.

[7] In Dresden gründete daraufhin der Jazzgitarrist Lothar Fiedler umgehend ein eigens Projekt mit dem Titel UND.

[8] Ein im Handel in der DDR übliches Schreibmaschinenpapierformat.

[9] Diejenigen, die unsere Initiative zur Kenntnis und zum Anlass für eigene Projekte nahmen, nannte diese von Beginn an Monatsschrift, Zeitschrift usw..

diente? Oder gab damals und gibt heute noch jedes so entstandene Heft Auskunft über seine Zeit und deren Verhältnisse? Es gab Klärungsbedarf in schwierigem gesellschaftlichen Umfeld. Ein Resultat: Zensur nein! Diskussionen allemal! Im Grunde stellte bereits das Prinzip der Einladung zur Mitarbeit eine Form der Auswahl dar.

Die ersten Ausgaben sind als formal völlig offen zu beschreiben. Darin spiegelte sich auch die Suche im offenen Feld. Dabei spielte die Fotografie schnell eine wichtige Rolle, wobei sie von der *street photography* über subjektive Fotografie bis zu konzeptuellen Auffassungen reichte. Grundsätzlich waren Beiträge bildender Künstler ab der dritten Ausgabe nicht mehr wegzudenken.

Als sich im Sommer 1984 herumsprach, dass ein technisches Denkmal in Ostberlin[10] gesprengt werden sollte, entstand von uns spontan als Protest außer der Reihe eine Sonderausgabe[11] zu diesem Vorgang.[12] Wir waren damit Teil eines breiten, durch alle gesellschaftlichen Schichten gehenden Widerstands.[13] Die Sprengung konnte dennoch nicht aufgehalten werden. Die Sprengungsfotos wurden für die Ausgabe nachgereicht. Dies kennzeichnete den Beginn zweier, verschiedener herausgeberischer Sachverhalte: Zum einen war damit das Feld der Sonderausgaben eröffnet und zum anderen, wenn auch mit leichter Verzögerung bis ins Jahr 1986, zogen nun thematische Ausgaben bei ENTWERTER/ODER ein.[14] Ein Thema bot einen äußeren

---

[10] Die einhundert Jahre alten, aus Backstein gemauerten Gasometer-Hüllen im Prenzlauer Berg standen auf der Denkmalliste Ostberlins und sollten dennoch gesprengt werden.

[11] *INTERIM. Zur Sprengung der denkmalgeschützten Gasometer*, Ostberlin Juli 1984,1. Sonderheft.

[12] Die Ausgabe liegt heute unter anderem im Prenzlauer Berg Museum in Berlin als einziges Zeugnis dieses Geschehens.

[13] Heute wissen wir, dass die Stasi über die Breite der Kritik sehr irritiert war. Der Protest war nicht mehr nur auf eine kleine Gruppe beschränkt.

[14] Bis 1990 erschienen 9 Sonderausgaben, bis 2022 waren es insgesamt 28 Sonderausgaben.

Rahmen, ein Spiel mit diversen Aussagen und auch eine Herausforderung für Autoren und Künstler.[15] Um offen zu bleiben und auch weil themenbezogenes Arbeiten nicht bei allen Künstlern auf Gegenliebe stieß, ließen wir thematische Ausgaben mit völlig freien Ausgaben sich abwechseln.

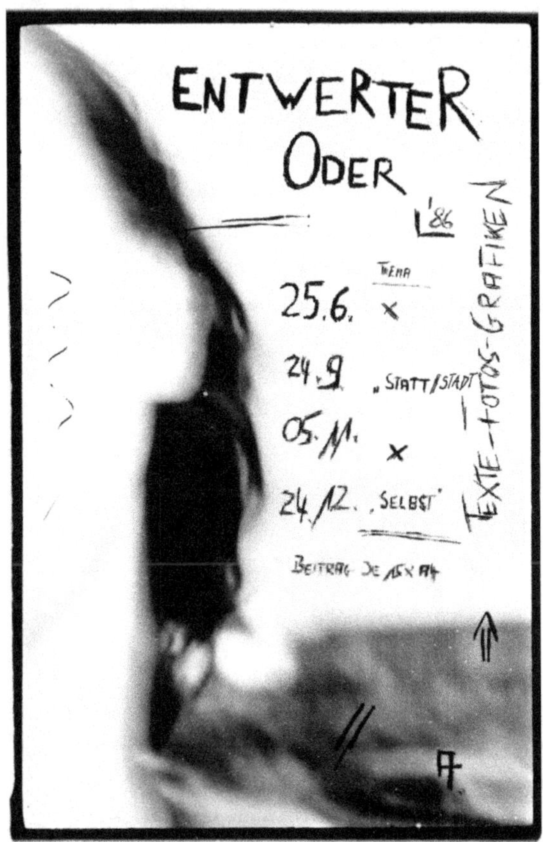

Bild 3: Entwerter/Oder Terminkärtchen, 1986

---

[15] Die Themen (Auswahl): statt stadt, selbst, berliner mauern, Parodien, konkrete+visuelle+experimentelle poesie, Musik, Tapetenwechsel, einzig & einsam, Es war einmal …, Gewalt, LTI/LQI, OV „Stasi", T/ERROR, unterwegs u.v.m.

Was von Anfang an eingeführt und bis heute konsequent durchgehalten wurde, war die Produktionsweise. Autoren wurden angesprochen und um Texte gebeten. Die Auflage dieser Texte stellte jeder selber her und übergab sie mir.[16] Es waren immer Erstveröffentlichungen. Genauso verfuhren die Künstler. Sie schlugen mir Arbeiten vor und produzierten die Auflage selbst. Bei den Arbeiten handelte es sich immer um signierte Originalarbeiten.[17] Die Auflage war zuvor bekannt gegeben und die Anzahl der Beteiligten entsprach der Auflagenhöhe. Ich stellte die Ausgabe zusammen. Die unterschiedlichen Inhalte, Aussagen und Materialien mussten durch eine visuell reizvolle Abfolge in einen sinnvollen Zusammenhang gebracht werden. Das war ein längerer, mitunter nicht einfacher Prozess. Da war viel Fläche von Nöten, um alles nebeneinander ausbreiten zu können und immer wieder neu zu kombinieren. Am Ende gab es immer eine Lösung. Schlussendlich organisierte ich das Buchbinderische.[18] Jeder Teilnehmer erhielt nach Fertigstellung eine Ausgabe. Wenn einzelne Exemplare übrigblieben, tauschte ich diese mit Ausgaben anderer Zeitschriftenprojekte. So entstand Stück für Stück eine interessante Sammlung.[19] Begleitet wurde diese Arbeit durch Wohnungslesungen, Jubiläumsfeiern,[20] Wochenend-Ausstellungen usw..[21]

---

[16] Dies geschah in den 1980er Jahren zumeist mit der Schreibmaschine, Kohlepapier und Durchschlägen.

[17] Fotografie, Zeichnung, Collage, Assemblage, Siebdruck, Linolschnitt, Holzschnitt, Radierung, Lithografie usw.

[18] Den Ausgaben, deren Umfang zwischen 60 und 80 Blättern maß, lagen auch Einladungen, gelegentlich Musikkassetten u.ä.m bei.

[19] In meinem Besitz: Entwerter/Oder, UND, U.S.W., usf., Mikado, schaden, *ariadnefabrik*, Anschlag, Zweite Person, LIANE, Herzattacke, Verwendung, Spinne, common sense, UNI/vers(;), Reizwolf, Gehen wir doch zum Strand, Glasnot, 1 Mose 2. 25, Sergej Bubka, Bizarre Städte.

[20] *Der 20. ENTWERTER/ODER*: Abendausstellung in einer leerstehenden Wohnung am 08.03.1986.

[21] *Letzte deutsche Herbstsalon*. Wohnungsausstellung zum Totensonntag, November 1984.

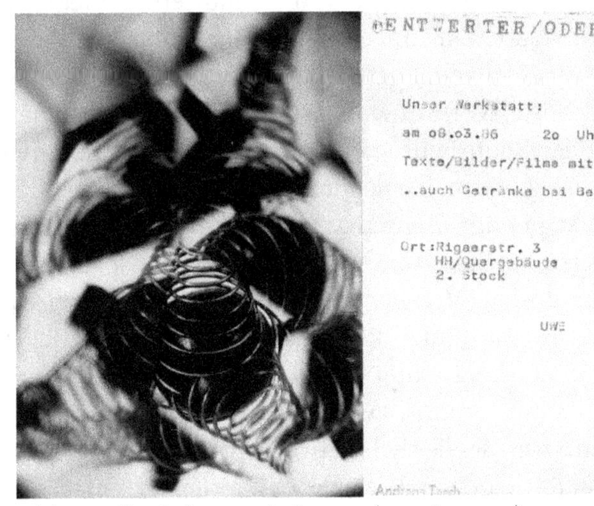

Bild 4 (links): Einladung (Vorderseite) zum Fest für Entwerter/Oder Nr. 20 in einer leerstehenden Wohnung, Ostberlin 1986, Foto: Andreas Tesch

Bild 5 (rechts): Einladung (Rückseite) zum Fest für Entwerter/Oder Nr. 20 in einer leerstehenden Wohnung, Ostberlin 1986.

Schaut man sich die Sonderausgaben an, so erweiterten sie die künstlerischen Möglichkeiten des Publizierens. Das war uns damals schon klar. Nun konnte auch eine kleine Gruppe von Künstlern oder ein Einzelner allein eine Ausgabe vorschlagen, bestimmen und herausgeben. Besonders auffällig sind hier die 6 Sonderausgaben zur Fotografie. Hierin zeigt sich auch ein besonderes Interesse des Herausgebers.

Es ging bei allem Tun immer um die selbstbestimmte Entscheidung und Freiheit des Publizierens und Experimentierens. Probieren, Ausprobieren schließt ein Scheitern nicht aus. Aber ich bot immer die Möglichkeit es zu versuchen. Ökonomisch war das kein Problem, da sich der Investitionsaufwand in Grenzen hielt (niemand sprach in solchen Begriffen). Kommerzielle Gedanken spielten hierbei ohnehin keine Rolle. Wir produzierten nicht für einen Markt. Wir tauschten uns aus und behaupteten mit unseren Aktivitäten einen eigenen gesellschaftlichen Raum und warteten ab, was nun passierte. Wenn nichts passierte, gingen wir einen Schritt weiter und der Raum wurde erweitert. Das Politische unseres Tun bestand darin, aus dem Dialog mit dem obrigkeitlichen Staat, der immer zuerst gefragt werden wollte und dann genehmigte oder verbot, ausgetreten zu sein. Wir haben nicht erst darum gebeten etwas tun zu dürfen. Wir haben es einfach getan. Dabei waren wir nicht naiv. Es war uns klar, dass dies von staatlicher Seite wahrgenommen, beobachtet wurde. Wir waren jung, wir waren frech, wir waren mutig. Was wir taten, und damit sichtbar einforderten, war schließlich das normalste von der Welt. Wir suchten unseren eigenen Weg. Dabei verließen wir das Kollektiv und standen zu unserem subjektiven Ausdruck. ENTWERTER/ODER war ein Medium in diesem Prozess; ein Medium zur Kommunikation junger Künstler.

Die Akteure dieser Szene kannten sich alle; einige mehr, andere weniger. Der Austausch unter den Protagonisten der Zeitschriften war sehr unterschiedlich. Einige arbeiteten enger zusammen, andere tauschten sich gelegentlich aus, manche gar nicht. Einige Autoren versuchten durch die Mitarbeit an mehreren Projekten auf diese Weise Brücken zu schlagen, was ohne Resonanz blieb. Da die einzelnen Projekte auch inhaltlich eigene ästhetische Überzeugungen und Wege verfochten, waren die Interessensgebiete abgesteckt. Es gab sicher auch Konkurrenzdenken, Ablehnungen und Unverständnis, aber keine Missgunst. Veranstaltungen, wie die erste Überblickausstellung aller Zeitschriften in der Samariterkirche in Ostberlin 1986, *wort und werk*,[22] oder die Veranstaltungsreihe *Zellinnendruck*,[23] anlässlich der Frühjahrsmesse 1990 in Leipzig, wurden selbstverständlich gemeinsam durchgeführt.

---

[22] *wort und werk*, organisiert von Peter Böthig und Christoph Tannert, Ostberlin, Juni 1986.
[23] *Zellinnendruck*, Leipzig, März 1990.

Die Zeitschriftenmacher waren dabei Teil einer sehr breiten Szene, deren Aktivitäten von Lesungen und Ausstellungen, Punk-Konzerten, Puppenspiel- und Theateraufführungen, Filmabenden und Festen in Wohnungen, Ateliers, Dachboden, Hinterhöfen reichte. Vieles lief im privaten Rahmen. Doch auch einige Vertreter des offiziellen, staatlich finanzierten Kulturbetriebes setzten sich für diese junge Szene ein. So gab es Auftritte in kleinen Klubs, kommunalen Kulturhäusern oder staatlichen Galerien. Häufig lief das glimpflich ab. Es kam vor, dass gelegentlich eine Veranstaltung kurzfristig abgesagt oder verboten wurde. Fand aber so ein offizieller Auftritt statt und sorgte dieser im Nachhinein für großes Aufsehen, Diskussionen und Auseinandersetzungen, konnte es passieren, das der Verantwortliche seinen Job verlor oder versetzt wurde. Das war von Übel, wurde aber in Kauf genommen. Es kostete nie den Kopf.

Im März 1987 erhielt ich eine Postkarte von der Sächsischen Landesbibliothek Dresden. Mir wurde mitgeteilt, dass die Bibliothek ein Interesse hätte, Ausgaben von ENTWERTER/ODER zu erwerben. Was wollten, was sollten wir tun? Wenn wir an eine öffentliche Bibliothek verkaufen würden, das war uns klar, hätte jeder unkompliziert Zugang zu den Ausgaben. Jeder! Also auch die Sicherheitsorgane. Da wir unsere Arbeit nicht als konspirativ verstanden, also kein Geheimnis daraus machten, beschloss ich, auf das Angebot einzugehen. Ich versuchte allerdings sicherzustellen, dass nach dem Ankauf die Ausgaben nicht im sogenannten 'Giftschrank'[24] verschwanden, sondern tatsächlich allen die es wünschten, zugänglich gemacht wurden.

---

[24] Bezeichnung für einen speziellen Bereich der Bibliotheken, wo Literatur verwahrt wurde, zu der der Leser eine besondere Lesegenehmigung benötigte.

Bild 6: Entwerter/Oder Nr. 75, Berlin 2000
Umschlag von Ottfried Zielke (1936–2016)

In der Wendezeit, 1989/90, tauchte die Frage auf, ob diese Arbeitsweise unter den neuen, ganz anderen gesellschaftlichen Rahmenbedingungen überhaupt noch Sinn machte. Alles wurde durch die anhaltenden Transformationsprozesse infrage gestellt. Die Türen für gänzlich andere technologische Verfahren, Druckprozesse, Auflagenhöhen, Vertriebswege, Internationalisierungen, Messen usw. standen weit offen. Aber wollten wir das? Wäre das am Ende nicht eine komplett andere Arbeit und auch ein ganz anderes Produkt? Wenn wir aber dabeiblieben, welchen Platz könnte diese kleinauflagige, mit Originalen arbeitende Zeitschrift auch in der neuen Gesellschaft einnehmen? Gerade im Gespräch mit Künstlern in dieser Zeit offenbarte sich die Wichtigkeit und Notwendigkeit diese Medium. Sie bestärkten mich und betonten ihr anhaltendes Interesse an so einem Ort wie dieser Zeitschrift, den sie für ihre Ideen und Experimente weiterhin bräuchten. So entwickelte sich das Projekt auch über 1990 hinaus zu einem Forum des Austausches und der Interaktion in dem Visuelle Poesie, Konzeptkunst und Fotografie wesentliche inhaltliche Säulen waren.[25] Auch nachdem ich einen Verlag gegründet hatte, stellte ENTWERTER/ODER die Basis meiner verlegerischen Arbeit dar.[26] Die Zeitschrift bot die Gelegenheit, junge Künstler und Autoren selbst und ihre Arbeiten und Texte näher kennenzulernen und eventuell zu Editionen oder Büchern weiterzuentwickeln.

Mittlerweile sind verschiedene Ausgaben von ENTWERTER/ODER in 48 Bibliotheken im In- und Ausland zu sehen. Die diesbezüglich umfangreichsten Sammlungen sind in der SLUB — Dresden,[27] Museum Schloss Burgk, der Anna-Amalia-Bibliothek Weimar und dem Deutschen Literaturarchiv Marbach zu sehen.

Bild 7: Entwerter/Oder Nr. 101, Berlin 2021
Umschlag: Uwe Warnke + Harald Weller

Obwohl ich immer noch mit der Kunst arbeite, publiziere und ediere, bin ich doch, ob ich will oder nicht, zu einem Zeitzeugen geworden. Solange das nicht als das Ende aller sonstigen Aktivitäten verstanden wird, geht das in Ordnung. Während ich immer noch mit Buchkunst, Fotografie, Editionen und Malerbüchern handele, kuratiere ich heute gemeinsam mit weiteren Kollegen Ausstellungen

---

[25] Ich erhielt 1991 den V. O. Stomps-Preis der Stadt Mainz für eine klein-verlegerische Leistung.

[26] 1990, Uwe Warnke Verlag, Berlin; spezialisiert auf Buchkunst und uni-kate Malerbücher; www.uwe-warnke.de.

[27] Sächsische Staats-, Landes- und Universitätsbibliothek Dresden.

zeitgenössischer Fotografie und erarbeite Kataloge, Symposien usw..[28] ENTWERTER/ODER ist dabei immer noch lebendig.[29]

Bild 9: Uwe Warnke, 'Dangerous Creations' roundtable discussion

---

[28] *Poesie des Untergrunds. Die Literaten- und Künstlerszene Ostberlins 1979-89, Berlin 2009; Geschlossene Gesellschaft. Künstlerische Fotografie in der DDR 1949-1989, Berlin 2012; In einem anderen Land. Transformationsprozesse an Beispielen zeitgenössischer Fotografie, Berlin 2018; Von Menschen und Mauern. 30 Jahre Mauerfall, Berlin 2019; Diversität der Moderne. 100 Jahre Groß-Berlin, Berlin 2020.*

[29] Bis heute, Mai 2022, sind 101 Ausgaben und 28 Sonderausgaben erschienen; www.entwerter-oder.de.

Zur *ariadnefabrik* und dem Milieu-spezifischen Zwielicht, in dem sie produziert wurde

Andreas Koziol

'The past is a foreign country. They do things different there.', heißt es in dem Roman 'The Go-Between' von L. P. Hartley. Der Aphorismus impliziert die Warnung, beim Erinnern von selbsterlebter Vergangenheit nicht allzu selbstgewiß zu sein. Die DDR wurde von vielen ihrer Bewohner schon damals als ein fremdes Land empfunden. Insofern gleicht eine Rückschau nicht nur der Einwanderung in ein fremdes Land, man trifft dort auch auf sich selbst als einen sich im sogenannten eigenen Land fremd fühlenden Fremden. 'They do things different there.' – das ist ebenfalls im doppelten Sinn zu verstehen, weil das Selbstverständnis der damaligen Untergrund-Künstler die Überzeugung beinhaltete, dass sie 'anders' waren.

Das Konzept der Andersartigkeit hatte sich von selbst ergeben, es war aus der Normopathie der real existierenden Verhältnisse als alternative Idee hervorgegangen. Junge Leute, die während der 70er Jahre des vorigen Jahrhunderts allmählich erwachsen wurden, hatten Grund sich zu fragen, was mit einem Leben in einem Staat anzufangen wäre, der ihre Entwicklungsmöglichkeiten von ihrer Bereitschaft zur Unterwerfung unter seine doktrinären Maßgaben abhängig machte. Kam Unterwerfung nicht in Frage, gab es eigentlich nur zwei Alternativen: Entweder Flucht oder Ausreise in den Westen, oder die Schaffung kreativer Spiel- und Freiräume im Schatten der autoritären Systemfassaden. Heiner Müller verglich einmal den SED-Staat der letzten zehn Jahre seines Bestehens mit der katholischen Kirche: Wer die (ideologischen) Dogmen nicht angriff, wurde von der Macht weitgehend in Ruhe gelassen. Damit hatte der

Dramatiker die Optionen relativer Freiheit in einem unfreien Land ganz gut umschrieben.

Dass man darin eingesperrt war wie in einem Gefängnis, ließ sich zwar nicht leugnen, doch da man die Gegebenheiten kannte, konnte man Wege finden und gehen, die nicht zwangsläufig gegen stets die gleiche Wand oder Mauer laufen mußten. Diese innere und apolitisch zu nennende Einstellung wurde freilich nicht von allen akzeptiert, es bildete sich seit den späten 70er und frühen 80er Jahren auch eine politisch motivierte Opposition gegen den Staat. Deren Treffpunkte deckten sich anfangs mit den Produktions- und Veranstaltungsräumen der Künstler; man fand sich gemeinsam zu Dichterlesungen in Ateliers und privaten Wohnungen ein und zelebrierte einen konspirativen Konsens, dem immer auch etwas Paranoides anhaftete. Denn es war ganz unmöglich, bei Zusammenkünften nicht mit der Anwesenheit von Stasispitzeln zu rechnen. Und aus den nach dem Zusammenbruch der DDR offengelegten Stasi-Akten ging hervor, dass jede konspirative Vorsicht zwecklos war, wenn der Feind sich als Freund mit dem gleichen Ekel vor Bespitzelungen maskierte.

Im Zuge der berechtigten Empörung über den Verrat in den ehemals eigenen Reihen gerieten die Kriterien der Unterscheidung von Kunst und Leben etwas durcheinander, indem beispielsweise behauptet wurde, dass sich die lyrischen Produkte eines Dichters, der sich als Denunziant entpuppte und also moralisch versagt hatte, dennoch weiterhin mit ästhetischem Gewinn lesen ließen. Wie das gehen sollte, entzieht sich meiner Erfahrung. Mir gelang es nie wieder, Gedichte etwa von Rainer Schedlinski und Sascha Anderson zu lesen und dabei ihren Verlust an menschlicher Glaubwürdigkeit auszublenden. Ich halte die Frage, ob ein fleißiger Stasispitzel nicht auch ein guter Dichter sein könne, für eine Einladung zu sophistischer Selbstquälerei und daher nicht für eine Verhandlungssache.

Der Name der Zeitschrift *ariadnefabrik* stammte übrigens aus dem Gedicht 'brunnen, randvoll' von Sascha Anderson. Es endet mit den Worten: 'schrei aus dem / fundament, geste aus staub / im gedächtnis, wandernde zone des irren gelächters / ariadnefabrik.' Dass der Initiator und Herausgeber Rainer Schedlinski (1956 – 2019) ebenfalls ein Stasi-Informant war, bezeichnet die tragische Komponente meiner Mitherausgeberschaft sowie jene der Mitwirkung zahlreicher Autoren. Der Slawist Fritz Mierau (1933 – 2018) meinte vor rund 30 Jahren einmal sinngemäß, dass er den Wert der *ariadnefabrik* nicht beschädigt sähe, die Zeitschrift sei trotz der Korruptheit ihres Herausgebers in erster Linie ein geistig unabhängiges Unternehmen gewesen. Der Glaube, sich der Kontrolle durch den Machtapparat entziehen zu können, habe sich zwar als Illusion erwiesen, doch habe das Heft in den drei Jahren seines regelmäßigen Erscheinens als zensurfreies Publikationsorgan am Rand der printmedialen Öffentlichkeit so gut funktioniert, wie es unter den Bedingungen der Diktatur möglich gewesen sei. Seiner wohlwollenden Einschätzung konnte ich damals nicht zustimmen, weil die Enttäuschung über den Verrat noch zu groß war.

Die Erkenntnis, ausgerechnet unter dem intentionalen Vorzeichen der Unabhängigkeit und Selbstbestimmung unwissentlich mit einem Zuträger der Stasi zusammengearbeitet zu haben, wollte sich nicht so bald verdauen lassen. Folgendes kam noch hinzu: Der Ungeist der geheimdienstlichen Zersetzungsstrategie überlebte seine Enthüllung. Sowohl Anderson als auch Schedlinski zeigten sich nicht sonderlich überzeugt von der Verwerflichkeit ihres Denunziantentums. Sie brachten das Kunststück fertig, die Trümmer des Vertrauens in ihre menschliche Zurechnungsfähigkeit im Fundament eines neu gegründeten Verlags zu versenken. Der Verlag, das 'Druckhaus Galrev' wurde eigentlich nur deshalb aufgebaut, um den initiatorischen Schwung der künstlerischen Selbstverlag-Aktivitäten vor dem Fall der Berliner Mauer mit nunmehr professionellen Mitteln fortzusetzen. Die übrigen Mitbegründer wußten in den ersten beiden Jahren nach der Gründung noch nicht, dass sie mit zwei ehemaligen Stasispitzeln unter einem Dach arbeiteten. Als diese Wahrheit dann endlich ans Licht der Öffentlichkeit kam, hätte sie theoretisch ein Sprengstoff sein müssen, der entweder die Verräter hinausfegte oder das neue

Haus zum Einsturz brächte. Aber es geschah weder das eine noch das andere. Die Verräter weigerten sich zu gehen, und die Verratenen hatten bereits zu viel Arbeit und Geld in das Galrev-Projekt investiert, um einfach alles hinwerfen und sich ein neues Betätigungsfeld suchen zu können. Erst im Laufe eines längeren Zeitraums wurde das Dilemma sozusagen seiner selbst müde, die Mehrzahl der Mitbegründer löste sich nach und nach aus dem Gesellschaftsvertrag des Verlagsunternehmens und ging ihrer eigenen Wege.

Zum Schluß vielleicht noch ein paar allgemeine Sätze zum Thema der Subversivität: In den engen Grenzen der DDR hatte das Subversive als Methode der Unterwanderung zwei sehr verschiedene Gesichter. Es gab durchaus so etwas wie semantische Subversivität, sie fand sich bei sprachspielerisch motivierten Dichtern. Deren Subversivität bestand darin, dass sie die Sprache der Macht entweder dekonstruierten oder naiv beim Wort nahmen und damit *ad absurdum* führten. Doch auch die Macht verstand sich auf subversive Strategien. Erschütterte die experimentelle Dichtung das Vertrauen in sprachliche Konventionen, so erschütterte die Macht mit ihrer gespenstischen Stasi-Praxis das Vertrauen der Menschen untereinander. Die sich an diesem Punkt mit einer gewissen Unvermeidlichkeit aufdrängende Frage, welche Methode die wirksamere gewesen war, ist meines Erachtens unzulässig, das Diabolische daran nötigt mich dazu, sie gleich wieder zurückzunehmen.

Gedichte

von

Uwe Kolbe

Gedicht des Christian mit der Amsel

Dunkeles Feuer.
Bote des Willens.
Es tagt. Es tagt.
Die Wirbel der Sprache:
beherrschst sie, kleine
begabte, singende Mutter.
Das Quellen der Töne:
beherrschst es, düstres
Talent du, lauthals mein Vater.
Botin des Alls
und furchtsamer Bote.
Trügrischer Lauthals.
Klagende Tochter.
Verführung des Morgens.
Tambour des Lichtes.
Es tagt. Es tagt.
Der Einbruch der Bläue.
Die Ankunft des Roten.
Das goldene Reich.
Ein Tag ist nie ein anderer.
Gewöhnliches Tier.
Mein Zeichen, der Liebe.
Rebellisches Zeichen.

Ein Gruß

In den Zügen kommt, auf den Straßen galoppiert, über
die Weinberge fliegt, durch die schlammigen Flüsse
schnellt, über Kirchen und Domtürme schreitet die
heidnische Gottheit,
die Schwester eine Gottes, der Bruder eines Gottes.
Wir sollten die Feuer entzünden.
Wir sollten singen auf den Bergen.
Wir sollten uns diesen Höllenspaß erlauben, die kargen
Masken hinzureichen in den Ämtern, hinzuwerfen vor
die Ämter in allen Städten und Flecken.
Wir sollten jene Sprache wieder erlernen, die vor den
Gazetten und Kameralügen lag, sich den Bauch hielt
und lachte.
Ich bin nur einer der Boten.
Kommt, laßt uns lästern die Prediger des Wassers.
Wir lachen sie kaputt.

Erwachsen zu sein

Was ist schön daran, erwachsen zu sein?
Gut, es gibt dieses und jenes, das schön ist,

doch einmal, in einer Sommernacht
- die Luft steht still, es ist fast so heiß

wie am Tag, und sie, für die dein Herz
schlägt, schläft, atmet ruhig – da also

hellwach, du hast gelesen, legst das Buch
aus der Hand, gehst an den Kühlschrank

und schenkst dir Weißwein in ein Glas,
es beschlägt sofort, du nimmst das Buch

wieder zur Hand und fährst fort zu lesen,
Gedichte, wirkliche, echte Gedichte.

Zu wissen, was echte Gedichte sind,
das ist schön daran, erwachsen zu sein.

Image: Aoife Ní Chroidheáin and Uwe Kolbe at Kolbe's poetry reading in the Main Lecture Hall, Taylor Institution Library.

Part Three

Samizdat in Oxford

Poster-making Workshop and Poetry Competition
Aoife Ní Chroidheáin

In the lead up to the 'Dangerous Creations' roundtable discussion, three special initiatives took place in order to shed light on the 'samizdat' printing phenomenon of East Germany in the 1980s.

The first of these events was a lecture in Hilary term entitled 'Stasi and Samizdat: power, authority and the unofficial magazines of the GDR'. This lecture explored how these unofficial magazines began life as an alternative outlet for those young artists forbidden from publishing in the highly regulated public sphere. The lecture provided an overview of how these magazines created and sustained an alternative public sphere under Communism for a network of artists, musicians and writers that gave them a sense of identity and solidarity in often dangerous situations.

Building on the theoretical knowledge of 'samizdat' from the lecture, all attendees of the lecture were invited to a 'samizdat' printing workshop at the Bodleian Library's Bibliographical Press with Professional Printer, Richard Lawrence.

This workshop, the second 'Dangerous Creations' event, provided students with the opportunity to select phrases and design motifs from an assortment of East Berlin's most famous 'unofficial' literary scene magazines and experimented with printing them using some of the Bodleian's historical hand-presses.

The third initiative was a poetry competition aimed at undergraduates. Students were invited to submit up to two poems (in English or in German) not exceeding 40 lines in length on the subject of secrecy as part of this competition. The competition attracted many entries, the prospect of being published in this volume alongside German poet, Uwe Kolbe undoubtedly a major attraction. The four winning entries are featured in this section and are testament to the remarkable poetic talent of three up-and-coming poets at the University of Oxford.

The final section of this publication highlights the fruits of the extraordinary creative collaboration that took place between students, both at the lecture and at the poster-making workshop, while also showcasing the literary talents of our poetry competition winners

'Samizdat' Student Poetry Competition

Natalie Perman, Clara Wittmann & Haley Flower

fotothek of doktor zhivago
Natalie Perman
St John's, Oxford

i
„ein nicht Türöffnen können
ein Stein in der Dunkelheit
da das andere Fremde nicht erreicht werden kann"
– „Das Luftholen dazwischen..", Schaden (10)

ii
the lights shine on a cello recital
the conductor's baton flies ton ab!
down into the city's stomached districts.
you've been told someone is dying,
or close to it. a man whispers: hör den
kleinsten Schall im Ohr. there is a kind
of poetry, but a poor one; boy meets tractor
and gets lost in an elevator.

iii
around the corner the boarding house boys
hide puppets in the glovebox of trabis
and race circles in the dark. their yellow–eyed
orbit is like a satellite; noise scratching
at the door of an eardrum. the puppets'
wooden bodies rattle all night.

iv
under the red light of a stop bath
the governess buries 800 rubles
in a trunk in the forest. a tower
block roots and sprouts a single room.
as square as a cube of pineapple,
a dark bunker; squeeze it and it leaks
green in your palm.

v

listen close and you can hear the puhdys
throw stones at a man conjugating verbs.
loud-mouthed narcissists we are,
we spin the wheels of the Chair of St Peter
over a cassette tape. walls have long ceased
to exist in this city.

vi
our unspoken words clink like the rim of a glass
submerged underwater. a droplet on the fingertip
contains a frozen lake, a wounded body
of water.

Deine LYRIK ist nicht unsicher
Clara Wittmann
St Hilda's, Oxford.

In that KYRIL café the faces of those free
poets, those liberated poets released
from one censorship into another
called choice and abundance
So maybe not liberated?
not necessarily,
because in that other place
the secrets kept you intimately entangled
reliant and resilient
sicherheit in samizdat

they acted in shibboleths
ensuring protection through layers
of secrets published in the VERLAG
in the GALREV they now appear, here
eyes wide, unsure and timid
at hearing their words spoken,
published proud
wondering if they will stand up to vast openness
without the buffering blanket of secrecy
es sicher zu halten.

Shibboleth of existence
Clara Wittmann
St Hilda's, Oxford.

S ilent you faded away from concrete existence,
H indered in your belonging to the whole
'I nclusive' Germany,
B lighted by their inability to see what was there
B inding was the secrecy that made you intimately close.
O thers don't get that that was your everything
L ove existed there
E verything functioning
T ogether, goals reached in collective creativity
H ungry in expression

O nerous is the task of keeping that entire existence alive
F orbidden, too – what isn't seen is that it was

E ntirely complete in that censored way.
'X' over forbidden messages.
I mpenetrable censorship leading to the use of
S hibboleths, tells reveal each other now
T ender once that instant recognition has occurred
E volving into a space, alien, which speaks in your tongue.
N ascent belonging, learning to be free but
C ensing need for new secrecy, self-secrecy, perpetuating the
E xistence of shibboleth

Gedankenstrich
Haley Flower
Somerville, Oxford

- —

G   e   d   a   n   k   e   n   s   t   r   i   c   h

diese Seite ist leer – absichtlich freigelassen –

ihrer Ansicht nach – offensichtlich – ist nichts da

        geschrieben

schreiben ohne sch

      sc

       cc

        hh

         hhH

         HH

       reiben wie Stift auf PapieR

     er   Radier

    schweigen muss man schreiben

   das Schweigen im Strich

Gedanken nur im Stich

gelassen   ohne Gedankenstrich ist das Papier nicht frei

Freiheit nur mit Absicht

ohne Absicht ist das Papier nur   –   leer

Samizdat Poster Workshop
Aoife Ní Chroidheáin

Building on the theoretical knowledge of 'samizdat' from the 'Stasi and Samizdat' lecture, students were invited to a printing workshop at the Bodleian Library's Bibliographical Press with Graduate lecturer Aoife Ní Chroidheáin and Professional Printer, Richard Lawrence.

This workshop provided students with the opportunity to select phrases and design motifs from an assortment of East Berlin's most famous 'unofficial' literary scene magazines and experimented with printing them using some of the Bodleian's historical hand-presses.

Over the course of the afternoon, three groups of students gathered in the Bodleian and using a variety of printing techniques including, typewriting, copying and hand-printing, created three distinct samizdat style posters. The following pages showcase the three posters on which the students collaborated, and are testament to the dynamic community of practice which the workshop facilitated.

Poster 1: What Now?
Charlotte Copeman, Joseph Dobbyn, Luise Morawetz

Poster 2: Traumlos Schreiben
Clara Wittmann, Natalie Perman, Rachel Isaacs, Lucian Shepherd, Ciara Beale, Lucas Veltkamp

Poster 3: Gegen den Strom
Haley Flower, Alexandra Hartlein, Gwendoline Davenport, Elizabeth Hornsby, Ella Myers, Lily Sheldon

GEGEN
DEN
STROM
dangerous creations
A roundtable discussion (New College)
& Poetry reading with Uwe Kolbe (Taylor Library)
Organisers: Aoife Ní Chroidheáin & Karen Leeder
Oxford, 8th April 2022
SPACES ARE LIMITED AND WILL BE ALLOCATED ON A FIRST-COME, FIRST-SERVED BASIS.

WHAT
now?
dangerous creations
A roundtable discussion (New College)
& Poetry reading with Uwe Kolbe (Taylor Library)
Organisers: Aoife Ní Chroidheáin & Karen Leeder
Oxford, 8th April 2022
SPACES ARE LIMITED AND WILL BE ALLOCATED ON A FIRST-COME, FIRST-SERVED BASIS.

Traumlos
Schreiben
CANCELLED
Your answers: 1 2 3 4 5 6 7 8 9 10
dangerous creations
A roundtable discussion (New College)
& Poetry reading with Uwe Kolbe (Taylor Library)
Organisers: Aoife Ní Chroidheáin & Karen Leeder
Oxford, 8th April 2022
SPACES ARE LIMITED AND WILL BE ALLOCATED ON A FIRST-COME, FIRST-SERVED BASIS.

Exhibition Catalogue
Aoife Ní Chroidheáin

This is an edited version of the bibliographical catalogue which accompanied the exhibition of 'Dangerous Creations', held at the Taylor Institution Library on 8th April 2022. The exhibition, curated by me in collaboration with Emma Huber, the German Subject Librarian and Karen Leeder, was designed to take place in the Main Lecture Hall of the Taylor Institution Library in conjunction with the poetry reading by Uwe Kolbe.

Our intention was present an introduction to the body of scholarship that has been produced on this subject by the academics who were in attendance at the roundtable and place this in conversation with the original 'samizdat' magazines of the GDR. While only a snapshot of the vibrant literary and cultural sphere associated with the 'unofficial' scene in the GDR, the magazines on display nonetheless provided an insight into the scene's remarkable literary experiment.

The exhibition provided a space to showcase not only the development of the Taylor Institution Library's specialist GDR collection, but also the world-class holdings of the Taylor Institution Library and the Bodleian Library.

Image: part of the exhibition

Birgit Dahlke, *Papierboot. Autorinnen in der DDR – inoffiziell publiziert* (Würzburg: Königshausen und Neumann, 1997)

Guillermo Deisler, *UNI/vers (;) 1* (Halle/Saale: *samizdat*, 1988)

Frank Eckart, *Eigenart und Eigensinn: Alternative Kulturszenen in der DDR 1980-1990* (Bremen: Edition Temmen, 1993)

Wolfgang Emmerich, *Kleine Literaturgeschichte der DDR* (Leipzig: Aufbau, 1996)

Günter Feist, *Kunstkombinat DDR: Daten und Zitate zur Kunst und Kunstpolitik der DDR 1954-1990* (Berlin: Nishan, 1990)

Ronald Galenza and Heinz Havemeister (eds), *Wir wollen immer artig sein: Punk, New Wave, HipHop, Independent-Szene in der DDR 1980-1990* (Berlin: Schwarzkopf & Schwarzkopf, 1999)

Thomas Günther, Uwe Warnke, and Ingeborg Quaas (eds), *Poesie des Untergrunds: Katalog zur Ausstellung im Generalkonsulat der Bundesrepublik Deutschland* (Berlin: Edition Galerie auf Zeit, 2010)

Heinz Havemeister, Susanne Schleyer, Volker Handloik, and Michael Thulin (eds), *Liane 6* (Berlin: *samizdat*, 1989)

Jens Henkel and Sabine Russ-Sattar, *DDR 1980-1989: Künstlerbücher und Originalgrafische Zeitschriften im Eigenverlag: Eine Bibliografie* (Gifkendorf: Merlin, 1991)

Sara Jones, *The Media of Testimony: Remembering the East German Stasi in the Berlin Republic* (Basingstoke: Palgrave Macmillan, 2014)

——, *Complicity, Censorship and Criticism: Negotiating Space in the GDR Literary Sphere* (Berlin: De Gruyter, 2011)

Uwe Kolbe, Lothar Trolle and Bernd Wagner (eds), *Mikado, oder Der Kaiser ist nackt: Selbstverlegte Literatur in der DDR* (Darmstadt: Luchterhand, 1988)

Uwe Kolbe, *Vineta: Gedichte* (Frankfurt a.M.: Suhrkamp, 1998)

——, *Lietzenlieder: Gedichte* (Frankfurt a.M.: Fischer, 2012)

——, *Gegenreden: Gedichte.* (Frankfurt a.M.: Fischer, 2015)

Ann Komaromi, *Uncensored: Samizdat Novels and the Quest for Autonomy in Soviet Dissidence* (Illinois: Northwestern University Press, 2015)

Andreas Koziol and Rainer Schedlinski (eds), *Abriss der Ariadnefabrik* (Berlin: Galrev, 1990)

Karen Leeder, *Breaking Boundaries: A New Generation of Poets in the GDR* (Oxford: Clarendon Press, 1996)

—— (ed.), *Rereading East Germany: The Literature and Film of the GDR* (Cambridge: University Press, 2016)

—— (ed.), *From Stasiland to Ostalgie: The GDR Twenty Years After* (Leeds: Maney, 2009)

Alison Lewis, *A State of Secrecy* (Lincoln: University of Nebraska Press, 2021)

——, *Die Kunst des Verrats: der Prenzlauer Berg und die Staatssicherheit* (Würzburg: Königshausen & Neumann, 2003)

Georgina Paul (ed.), *An Odyssey for Our Time: Barbara Köhler's Niemands Frau* (Amsterdam: Brill, 2013)

——., *Perspectives on Gender in Post-1945 German Literature* (Rochester, N.Y.: Camden House, 2009)

Uwe Warnke (ed.), *Entwerter/Oder* 100 (Berlin, *samizdat*, 2016)

Josephine Von Zitzewitz, *The Culture of Samizdat: Literature and Underground Networks in the Late Soviet Union* (London: Bloomsbury, 2020)

Contributor Biographies

Aoife Ní Chroidheáin	Aoife Ní Chroidheáin is a doctoral student in her final year of study at the University of Oxford. She specialises in post–1945 German and Austrian literature. Her doctoral research focuses on the "samizdat" magazines of East Berlin in the 1980s. Alongside her doctoral study, Aoife is a Lecturer at Balliol College, Oxford where she teaches German literature.
Heinz Havemeister	Hans Havemeister, geb. 1958 in Eisenberg (Thüringen), Autor, Musiker, lebt in Berlin. 1982-1987 Studium der Kunstwissenschaft an der Humboldt-Universität zu Berlin. Ab 1988 Mitherausgeber der originalgrafischen Zeitschrift und Musik-Edition *LIANE*, Beiträge in inoffiziellen Zeitschriften. 1990 - 1993 Mitbegründer und Arbeit im Verlag Druckhaus Galrev. 1991-2012 Mitglied der Bolschewistischen Kurkapelle Schwarz-Rot, danach Mitglied der Sogenannten Anarchistischen Musikwirtschaft. Musikprojekt u.a.: Heinz & Franz, Miliz Christi, Die Liebe, Eigenrauschen. Mit Ronald Galenza Buchveröffentlichungen: „Wir wollen immer artig sein"(1999) und „Feeling B – Mix mir einen Drink" (2002).
Sara Jones	Sara Jones is Professor of Modern Languages at the University of Birmingham. Her research focuses on the history and memory of state socialism in Central and Eastern Europe, especially the GDR. She is author of three

monographs: *Complicity, Censorship and Criticism* (2011), *The Media of Testimony* (2014) and *Towards a Collaborative Memory* (forthcoming in 2022). She is Co-Investigator and Lead for the Literary Networks strand of the AHRC-funded project *Knowing the Secret Police*.

Uwe Kolbe

Uwe Kolbe, geboren 1957 in Berlin, lebt als freier Schriftsteller in Dresden. Neben diversen Gedichtbänden und Essays veröffentlichte er einen Roman ('Die Lüge', 2014). Von 1997 bis 2004 unterrichtete er Kreatives Schreiben an der Universität Tübingen. 2005 nahm er an dem internationalen Dichtertreffen 'Sailor's Home' in London teil (s.a. die Anthologie 'Sailor's Home' bei Shearsman Books). Zuletzt erschienen die gedichtbände 'Die sichtbaren Dinge' 2019 sowie 'Imago' 2020.

Ann Komaromi

Ann Komaromi is Associate Professor at the Centre for Comparative Literature and the Department of Slavix Languages and Literatures at the University of Toronto. She created the digital archive "Project for the Studey of Dissidence and Samizdat." Her book *Soviet Samizdat: Imagining a New Society* is forthcoming from NIU Press.

Andreas Koziol

Andreas Koziol, geb.1957 in Suhl/Thüringen, lebt in Berlin. In den 1980er Jahren Mitherausgeber der Ostberliner Untergrundzeitschriften „verwendung" und „ariadnefabrik"; seit 1990 zahlreiche Buch-, Heft- und Zeitschriftenveröffentlichungen mit Gedichten, experimenteller Prosa und

Essayistik, zuletzt „Nachgeblätterte Zeiten", Hamburg, 2020.

Karen Leeder

Karen Leeder is Professor of Modern German literature at the University of Oxford and teaches German at New College. Her first book was on poetry in the samizdat scheme: Breaking Boundaries (OUP, 1996). More recently she edited Rereading East Germany: The Literature and Film of the GDR (CUP, 2016). She is a prize-winning translator of contemporary German literature, including Durs Grünbein, Volker Braun and Ulrike Almut Sandig.

Alison Lewis

Alison Lewis is Professor Emeritus in German Studies at The University of Melbourne, Australia. She has published extensively on modern German literature, history, politics and culture. Her latest book is *A State of Secrecy: Stasi Informers and the Surveillance of Culture* (Potomac Books).

Ray Ockenden

Ray Ockenden joined Wadham College as its first Fellow in German in 1967, and has been teaching German literature and language for the University and for many other Oxford colleges ever since. At Wadham, where he is now an Emeritus Fellow, he has fulfilled several College offices, such as Dean, Senior Tutor and Sub-Warden, and he looked after the College cellar for 24 years; since 2003 he has been Wadham's Dean of Degrees. Ray's research work has been concerned with German literature, especially poetry, from 1750 to the present day. He has written about Geothe, especially his classical verse, and the later poetry of Brecht. His most recent publications have examined the work and influence of Stefan George, and aspects of the poetry of Mörike.

Susanne Schleyer

Susanne Schleyer, geb. 1963 in Eisenach/Thüringen, lebt in Berlin, Diplom in Kunst, Germanistik, Pädagogik an der Humboldt Universität zu Berlin; Diplom in Künstlerischer Fotographie an der Hochschule für Grafik und Buchkunst Leipzig bei Prof. Arno Fischer und Prof. Timm Rautert; Arbeit als freie Künstlerin und Fotografin; ab 1988 Herausgeberin der originalgrafischen inoffiziellen Zeitschrift *LIANE* u.a. mit Heinz Havemeister; Founderin und Arbeit im Buchverlag Druckhaus Galrev Berlin; ab 1999 künstlerische Zusammenarbeit mit Michael J. Stephan; Aufbau des Fotoarchiv autorensarchiv.de; längere Arbeitsaufenthalte in San Francisco/USA, Buenos Aires/Argentinien, Sankt Petersburg/Russland, Johannesbury/Südafrika; zahlreiche nationale und internationale Stipendien und Preise, seit 1990 regelmässig nationale und internationale Ausstellungen.

Tara Talwar Windsor

Tara Talwar Windsor specialised in German literary and cultural politics from the early 20th century to the present. She is currently Schröder Research Associate for Equality and Diversity in German Studies at the University of Cambridge and Postdoctoral Affliliate at Newnham College. From 2019-21, she was Research Fellow in the AHRC-funded project *Knowing the Secret Police*.

Uwe Warnke

Uwe Warnke is author, publisher and curator. He founded 1982 the first illegal original-graphic art-journal, called Entwerter-Oder, in East Berlin, GDR. Issue no. 101 was published in 2021. In recent years he has also been involved with contemporary photography and an extensive interview project on transformation processes in contemporary fine arts due to the challenges of social change in Germany in 1989/90.